Appraising Performance for Results

Second Edition

Appraising Performance for Results

Second Edition

Tom Philp

McGRAW-HILL BOOK COMPANY

London · New York · St Louis · San Francisco · Auckland
Bogotá · Caracas · Hamburg · Lisbon · Madrid · Mexico · Milan
Montreal · New Delhi · Panama · Paris · San Juan · São Paulo
Singapore · Sydney · Tokyo · Toronto

Published by
McGRAW-HILL Book Company (UK) Limited
Shoppenhangers Road, Maidenhead, Berkshire, England SL6 2QL
Telephone Maidenhead (0628) 23432
Fax 0628 770224   Telex 848484

British Library Cataloguing in Publication Data
Philp, Tom
  Appraising performance for results.—2nd ed
  1. Personnel. Performance. Assessment
  I. Title
  658.3'125
ISBN 0-07-707334-7

Library of Congress Cataloging-in-Publication Data
Philp, Tom
  Appraising performance for results/Tom Philp—2nd ed.
    p. cm.
  1. Employees—Rating of.   I. Title
  HF5549.5.R3P49   1990
  658.3'125—dc20
  ISBN 0-07-707334-7

2345 B & S 9321

Typeset by Rowland Phototypesetting Limited, Bury St Edmunds, Suffolk, and printed and bound in Great Britain by Billing and Sons Limited, Worcester

Contents

Acknowledgements

My thanks to my wife Barbara and my family and my friends for their help and tolerance.

Without question my thanks also go to Karen and her staff in our head office.

Sincere thanks must also go to my business partner, Neil Philp, who has brought so many fresh ideas on the subject of appraisal to my attention, not only in the training of people in appraisal techniques, but also in the design of appraisal documentation for our international client base.

Thanks to you all.

Introduction

Performance appraisal is the application of a number of skills, which managers are required to put into practice to maintain and improve the performance of all the people who report to them. In the interests of the company, the appraising manager, and the person being appraised, it is essential that the skills are applied professionally.

Before examining the specific skills which have to be developed in order that people can effectively appraise, it must be stressed that there are two distinct sets of circumstances where the skills have to be put into practice by all managers in any organization.

One set of circumstances will be encountered on a daily/ weekly, ongoing basis where any movement away from the required performance standard has to be looked at, with corrective action taken to rectify the situation: this is quite simply good management practice. It is after all, part of managers' responsibilities to monitor the performance of their staff to ensure that situations do not get out of control.

An analogy In successful manufacturing companies, it is accepted that it is more efficient and effective to monitor the quality of components while they are being manufactured. Any indication that components are approaching an unacceptable tolerance level allows adjustments to be made at the appropriate time; this ensures correct quality all the way through the process. If more managers took a lead from this sharp end of the business, and applied the same philosophy to the management of their people, they would be ensuring correct performance from all of their staff, all the year round. Surely this would be in the interests of all the people involved, not least of these being the customer.

The second set of circumstances requires the application of the skills in a more formalized way to satisfy the corporate requirements of the company. Normally an annual appraisal system is coordinated by a central personnel function for the purpose of assisting with manpower planning, and the provision of services to meet the training/development needs of the company. It is however the responsibility of each manager to conduct the annual appraisal, and good use of appraisal skills will ensure that the information gathered is correct, and that any actions required to be taken will be contributing to the overall improvement of the company's performance. In this context, annual appraisals can be described as an essential part of a company's quality control and stock-taking activities.

All that has been stated so far could easily be described as obvious, and mere common sense. Yet when discussing the subject of appraisals with several hundred managers every year, the comments received are very often extremely negative. By far the majority of managers interviewed say appraisals within their company produce no real value; in some instances they are actually described as counter-productive. Clearly the views expressed are genuine, but there are many different reasons for them, often a combination of attitudes, knowledge and skills. The most significant attitudinal factor, which appears to have the greatest impact in determining whether appraising people is productive or not, is linked to the individual manager's understanding of how to manage people for results.

In companies where there is a very high degree of professionalism with regard to the skills of people management, there is usually a positive attitude towards appraising performance. As a result it is not difficult to help managers to recognize, accept, develop and apply appraisal skills. When the improved results are observed, these managers will work at their newly acquired skills to maintain and improve them, thereby ensuring continued improvement all round. On the other hand, where companies employ managers who have not had the opportunity, willingness, and/or encouragement to apply good management practices, there can be a real reluctance by those managers to accept any approach which relies to a very great extent on openness, trust and objectivity. In fairness to these managers, it should be added that their reluctance will be compounded if the most senior managers in the company are from a similar mould.

The aims of this book are geared to improving the effectiveness of performance appraisal by the provision of very practical guidelines, which, when put into operation in your own job, and in your own way, will prove the benefits not only to yourself as the appraising manager, but also to the people who work for you, and your company as a whole. You will be able to derive maximum satisfaction from your job as a manager of people. This will all have the effect of strengthening your positive attitude towards appraisal, which in the end is the key to really effective improvements in performance. Performance appraisal is just one of the skills of a manager, but as with all skills success is dependent on being in the hands of a professional. Follow the guidelines for appraisal, make it a way of life and you will reap the benefits that are there for you and your employees, and for your company.

I.

The purpose and benefits of performance appraisal

Why there is a need for performance appraisal

In the business world investment is made in machinery, equipment and services. Quite naturally time and money is spent ensuring that they provide what their suppliers claim. In other words the performance is constantly appraised against the results expected.

When it comes to one of the most expensive resources companies invest in, namely people, the job of appraising performance against results is not very often carried out with the same objectivity, if indeed it is done at all! Quite apart from the fact that this is an extremely inefficient way to utilize a valuable resource, surely it is true that people in general do need to know:

- what is expected of them;
- how they are going to be measured; and
- how they are getting on.

The absence of this information simply contributes to increased frustration with the result of poor performance. The old adage that 'No news is good news' is not very often true—and in any event how will anyone know whether any improvement is being achieved?

During the years 1969 through to 1989 I have been fortunate enough to interview managers at all levels, from a wide range of industry and commerce, and in many countries in the world. One set of questions used on each occasion was: 'How often does your immediate manager (your boss) discuss the following with you?'

- your job objectives?
- areas where you are performing well?
- areas where you should improve your performance?
- your relationship with others?
- development plans for you?
- your views on problems you encounter?

The questions were chosen in the belief that they should frequently arise in discussions between people and their managers, and that the questions can also form a sound base for an effective appraisal interview.

From 5000 managers interviewed, the responses were:

- more than once per year   9%
- once per year   53%
- less than once per year   31%
- never   7%

This would seem to confirm that a large number of managers believe once a year to be often enough to sit down with their people in an attempt to make sure things are going well. This old-fashioned and unproductive attitude towards such an important part of a manager's responsibilities has to be changed, if improvements in a company's performance are to be achieved.

The most common reasons for unproductive attitudes

The attitudes of managers who are responsible for appraising others are mainly affected by the following:

1. A lack of willingness to accept ownership of the responsibility to appraise people—it is someone else's job.
2. A lack of acceptance of the fact that appraisal should be a natural part of a manager's day-to-day duties, as well as quarterly, biannual, or annual stock-taking activity.
3. Lack of skill or knowledge with regard to setting clearly defined standards of performance, with which to appraise against.
4. Lack of skill in separating that which is within the job holder's control as opposed to that which is not.
5. Failure to recognize and/or accept that the manager's own behaviour can influence a job holder to perform well or to perform badly.
6. A fear of discussing performance, when they have been accustomed to telling people what they thought.

Attitudes of the people being appraised are mainly affected by the following:

1. Suspicion of why they are being appraised.
2. Concern for fair appraisal.
3. The use of totally subjective measurements of performance.
4. Being appraised against personality traits rather than results.
5. The assumption by the manager that job holders are totally in control of their performance—the 'more-effort-needed' syndrome.
6. Very little happening, if anything, as a result of being appraised.
7. What use is a once-a-year event anyway?

A conscious effort to improve the way in which people are being appraised will provide many advantages to the company, the manager and the person being appraised—good reasons for making appraisal a way of life.

Another good reason for effectively appraising the performance of the people who report to you stems from the fact that as soon as one person receives payment for being responsible for others, that person is immediately being paid to appraise the performance of the others. It seems reasonable, therefore, to expect people to do what they are actually paid to do.

Most damage has been done to performance appraisal as a result of traditional approaches, which only concentrate on formalized schemes on the once-a-year basis.

Appraisal schemes first adopted by industry and commerce were adapted from the type of systems in use in the armed services. The principal purpose of such schemes is usually the evaluation of the individual in terms of salary, promotion or career development.

Schemes of this nature tend to concentrate on the evaluation of the characteristics of the individual being appraised rather than upon the results that the individual produces for the organization. Such schemes are often devoid of any consideration that there are factors influencing the performance that are either totally outside the individual's control, or induced by some other person or condition.

The tendency of this type of approach is to focus on the rating of subjective factors thought to be associated with successful performance. Often the terms used contain lists of descriptive words and/or phrases against which the assessor gives the individual a rating.

Typical descriptive terms used include:

- dependability
- initiative
- loyalty
- energy and application
- judgement and reliability

- leadership
- cooperation
- motivation
- attitude to work
- enthusiasm
- trustworthiness
- relations with other people

The disadvantages of this approach are numerous:

1. The terms themselves are extremely ambiguous. For instance, it is unlikely that any group of managers would share exactly the same interpretation of any of these terms. Of necessity any appraisal using these words will be extremely subjective, and as a result totally unfair. Most managers would opt for an 'average mark' in their assessment.

2. Because assessment in these terms deals with the individual rather than with the results that the individual produces for the organization, it is very difficult to communicate with the individual involved. The person being appraised is likely to see any critical assessment of this type as a personal attack. The factors deal with the emotive areas closely concerned with personality, and the majority of people will tend to react defensively.

3. Assessment in these terms does not provide any guidance on how to improve performance. Guidance, when given, tends to be of the pull-your-socks-up variety.

4. The assessment, having an emphasis on personality charac-teristics, tends to place a premium on conformity rather than on performance. The question tends to be 'Is this individual the sort of person we want in the organization?' rather than 'Does this individual produce the results that the organization requires from someone doing this job?'

5. The assessment fails to include any consideration of the effect which the manager's behaviour and attitude towards the person being appraised has on the situation. For example, total autocrats very seldom generate real cooperation, enthusiasm and loyalty in the people who report to them.

6. Where the assessment is used to reward or punish this can place considerable pressure on the appraising managers. They are aware of the effect an adverse assessment can have on the relationship with the job holder. For this reason some managers opt out of their responsibility to do any form of appraisal. If they are compelled to do it then the next option is to water down the assessment to avoid conflict with the individual being appraised.

On the other hand, of course, there are managers who seem to enjoy conflict situations. For example, one organization carried out an appraisal system involving an annual review where the results were communicated to the job holder. The manager invited the job holder into the office, with no advance notice, and the words used to the job holder were 'Come in, it's telling-off time, and it's your turn.'

Underlying many of these early approaches to appraisals were such assumptions as:

- Individuals cannot adequately determine for themselves whether they are doing a good job.
- Individuals are basically insecure and need constant reassurance as to how well they are doing and do not want to discuss areas where performance is down.
- Individuals have little to contribute in the field of their own development and the development of the organization.
- The appraising manager possesses all the information necessary to carry out effective and accurate appraisal of staff.

Changes in these assumptions must be made if appraisal is to be effective. These changes also mean that the purpose and methods of appraisal must be reviewed.

New approaches to performance appraisal

The appraisal of performance should be geared to:

- improving the ability of the job holder;
- identifying obstacles which are restricting performance;
- agreeing a plan of action which will lead to improved performance.

It is widely accepted that the most important factor in organizational effectiveness is the effectiveness of the individuals who make up the organization. If every individual in the organization becomes more effective, then the organization itself will become more effective. The task of reviewing situations and improving individual performance must therefore be a key task for all managers.

For appraisal to be effective, which means producing results for the company, each manager has to develop and apply the skills of appraisal. These are:

- *Setting standards* on the performance required, which will contribute to the achievement of specific objectives.

- *Monitoring performance* in a cost-effective manner, to ensure that previously agreed performance standards are actually being achieved on an ongoing basis.

- *Analysing any differences* between the actual performance and the required performance to establish the real cause of a shortfall rather than assume the fault to be in the job holder.

- *Interviewing*: having a discussion with the job holder to verify

7

the true cause of a shortfall, and developing a plan of action which will provide the performance improvement required.

Appraisal can then become a way of life, not concerned simply with the regulation of rewards and the identification of potential, but concerned with improving the performance of the company. The benefits of appraisal in these terms are immediate and accrue to the appraising manager, the subordinate manager/employee, and to the company as a whole.

The following examples taken from three different types of industry may serve as an indication of how easy it can be to realize real benefits by this approach.

CASE NO. I   A COMMERCIAL INDEPENDENT RADIO STATION

The life-blood of the commercial radio station is the extent to which advertising space can be sold. This is made easier to do, and more profitable for the advertisers, if the station can capture and maintain the right audience and increase the number of listeners in this pre-determined audience group.

When I was asked how to set standards of performance for the programme announcers, who were described as having to be very creative outgoing people, it did at first appear as if it would be difficult.

However, knowing that audience surveys were carried out in the industry, and that information was available by district and by times of the day, I asked if this could be used as a starting point even if the figures would not be all that reliable. The reply confirmed the availability of the information, but contradicted my assumptions on the unreliability of the figures which were said to be of proven reliability over the years.

With regard to using this information as a starting point for a standard of performance, it was said to be impractical as audience

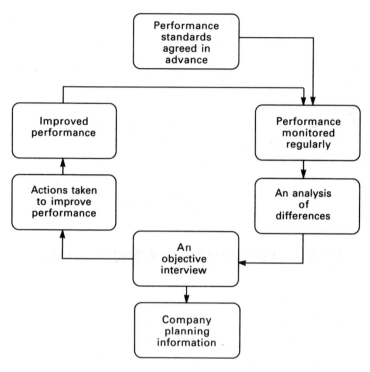

Resultant benefits

For the company
improved: Efficiency
Profitability
Training needs
Manpower planning
Quality of service
Salary administration
Performance of the company

For the manager
improved: Relationships
Communication
Decision making
Removal of problems
Individual performance
Departmental performance
Performance of the manager

For the job holder
improved: Relationships
Communication
Self-confidence
Job satisfaction
Removal of obstacles
Understanding of role
Performance of job holder

Figure 1.1   A model for effective performance appraisal

figures by shift were not made available to the announcers. Apparently the reasons for this were to do with concerns about unfair competition between announcers, and about successful announcers becoming over-confident in themselves. This first area of concern, the one of possible unfair competition, is very important. None the less the problem is not too difficult to overcome as competition is only unfair when differing circumstances are overlooked.

The second area of concern, the possibility of successful announcers becoming over-confident, is slightly more difficult to handle. In a job where creative outgoing people are needed, the effect of self-confidence is essential. However it is once again the possibility of unfair competition which can turn this self-confidence into over-confidence. For example, the announcers who had most experience, and were therefore best known, were given the shift in the most popular time of the day which potentially had the highest audience. Being successful in these circumstances is not always related to earned success.

By disclosing audience figures by shift, and also by considering all known related circumstances regarding each shift, a fair standard of improved performance for each shift was established. The next step was to arrange for regular feedback to the relevant announcers regarding their performance, which they could compare with the agreed standard for that shift.

The result of the actions of establishing fair standards of performance, and feeding results back to the relevant announcers on a weekly basis, was to allow all the announcers in this already successful company to achieve, to see, and to show improvements in their performance all round.

Specific benefits derived as a result of the actions

Benefits to the manager
- improved performance of individuals
- improved performance of department
- improved communication
- improved relationships
- identification of staff weaknesses
- identification of staff strengths
- identification of potential problems
- identification of departmental training needs
- identification of individual training needs
- identification of potential
- increased opportunity to communicate department/company objectives
- increased opportunity to praise
- more valid information relating to increased job satisfaction

Benefits to the job holder

- opportunity to find out about own strengths
- opportunity to discuss company/department objectives
- identification/clarification of own role
- improved working relationships
- increased job satisfaction
- improved self-confidence

Benefits to the company

- improved performance of individuals
- improved performance of departments
- improved profitability
- improved efficiency

- .improved quality of service
- increased ability to evaluate value of training provided
- more reliable information relating to manpower planning
- more accurate assessment of potential of individuals
- more able to adapt to short-term needs

CASE NO. 2 A LARGE SUPERMARKET IN THE FOOD INDUSTRY

One of the most important factors in determining success in this industry is the speed at which food can be moved from the suppliers to the customer at the counter. To do this efficiently requires extremely sophisticated systems, and high levels of skills in all of the people involved. Any failures will impact on customer satisfaction in the areas of quality of produce, non-availability, or inability to bring out new products ahead of the competition.

While discussing standards of performance with one group of managers involved in the buying and display of products it came to light that potential delays had inadvertently been built into the systems. The cause of this situation was a clash of responsibilities between two departments.

For example, although the managers were responsible for arranging the buying and delivery of the produce, they were also responsible for determining the correct display of the produce in the stores. They did not however have the authority to ensure that the allocated space was available when the produce arrived. Quite apart from the frustration experienced, there were occasions when deliveries would be made to the store at the time when adequate shelf space was not available.

The reason this situation came to the surface was the fact that we were looking at the total job of the managers and setting standards against all of the potentially high impact elements within the job. Previously, the success of the managers was measured by the difference between buying price and selling price. Some of the factors which controlled the profit margin did not get any recognition.

The identification and removal of obstacles which hinder the ultimate performance allows the company to reduce its hidden costs and thus become really profitable. Obstacles will seldom be recognized unless managers take the time to discuss the total job with the job holder, to find out what difficulties or problems the job holder experiences.

Specific benefits derived as a result of the actions

Benefits to the manager

- improved performance of individuals
- improved performance of department
- improved relationships
- identification of existing problems
- more valid information relating to increased job satisfaction
- more valid information relating to employees' attitudes
- another opportunity to demonstrate own managerial skills

Benefits to the job holder

- identification/clarification of own role
- improved working relationships
- increased job satisfaction
- improved self-confidence

Benefits to the company

- improved performance of individuals
- improved performance of departments
- improved profitability

- improved efficiency
- improved quality of service
- labour turnover information more valid
- more accurate assessment of potential of individuals
- more accurate assessment of potential of departments

CASE NO. 3   A MEDIUM SIZED DISTRIBUTION COMPANY

In this particular industry, the speed at which a supplier can react to a customer's requirements is vital.

The depot managers at the sharp end of the business are required to have a sound knowledge of their customers' and potential customers' requirements, their industry, the competition, and the procedures to which they have to adhere. A major difficulty this company was experiencing was that of a high turnover of depot managers, much higher than it should have been for that industry. Many managers left within six months of joining the company, others were dismissed even earlier. Trying to build up a bank of experience was a difficult task.

On joining the company, the only standard of performance the manager was given related to the value of revenue which the depot had to generate.

At monthly intervals, the depots would be visited by a senior manager to carry out what was referred to as an assessment of performance. Many items were included in the check-list; however, only two of these, namely sales revenue generated and timekeeping, gave any definition of what was expected. The rest were totally subjective.

Depot managers would either leave out of sheer frustration or they would be dismissed because of what was called a wrong attitude to work.

A simple list of the areas where results were expected, with these expanded into the related key tasks and associated standard of performance allowed the depot managers to know quite precisely what was expected. It also allowed the senior managers to monitor performance objectively and move away from the issues of personality.

Specific benefits derived as a result of the actions

Benefits to the manager

- improved performance of individuals
- improved performance of department
- improved communication
- improved relationships
- identification of staff weaknesses
- identification of staff strengths
- identification of existing problems
- identification of potential problems
- identification of individual training needs
- identification of development needs
- identification of potential
- find out areas in which to increase delegation
- increased opportunity to communicate department/company objectives
- increased opportunity to praise
- increased opportunity to correct
- more valid information relating to increased job satisfaction
- more valid information relating to training received
- more valid information relating to employees' attitudes
- another opportunity to demonstrate own managerial skills

Benefits to the job holder

- opportunity to find out about own strengths
- opportunity to find out about own weaknesses
- opportunity to discuss company/department objectives

- identification/clarification of own role
- improved working relationships
- increased job satisfaction
- improved self-confidence
- see relationship to training provided
- see relationship to development plans

Benefits to the company

- improved performance of individuals
- improved performance of departments
- improved profitability
- improved efficiency
- improved quality of service
- more reliable company training needs
- easier to budget for training costs
- increased ability to evaluate value of training provided
- more reliable information relating to manpower planning
- labour turnover information more valid
- more accurate assessment of potential of individuals
- more accurate assessment of potential of departments
- more able to adapt to short-term needs
- better able to plan and adjust salary scales where appropriate

2.

Setting performance standards

The first requirement for effective performance appraisal is a common understanding of the standard of performance in the job expected from each individual. This is often a difficult but essential task, if the business is to run successfully. After all, the success of the business itself is measured against standards such as profitability, cash flow, quality of the goods or services, sales, growth, and labour turnover for example. Each of these must be geared to and contribute to the overall success of the company.

When talking to people in industry and commerce it is apparent that the words 'standard of performance' can cause some nervousness. And yet consider for a moment what is meant by a standard of performance.

Think about your satisfaction in relation to the food you eat and drink, your visits to the cinema or theatre, your relationship with your wife/husband/friend, parents, children or other relatives, television/radio programmes, sports, hobbies or clothes. It is normal to know quite clearly the standard of performance sought. What makes work so very different?

Many managers often impose frustration on themselves with the excuse that they are not going to set standards because they impose restrictions and can cause conflict. Even if this is true, if you do not know how well your staff are performing it can be very frustrating indeed, especially when you are paying their salary from your budget.

On the other hand, if you are on the receiving end of this it can be even more frustrating not to know what is expected. Furthermore, if no one knows the standard of performance that is required, it can be said, quite truthfully, that any standard of performance will be acceptable! For example, if you arrange to bring in to your home someone to decorate a room for you, would you do this without agreeing a standard of finish required? It is possible that some people would think this to be unnecessary on the basis that the decorator would know, and you had both agreed, the estimate of costs. A reasonable assumption to make? Yes, of course it is, but what happens if you are dissatisfied with the finished result, and the decorator's account arrives through your door? A difficult argument at the least!

Recognizing the need for standards is one thing, knowing how to set them, and indeed which parts of the job to set them in, is another.

I can recall one particularly frustrated manager saying that he accepted that standards would be useful, but that it would not work in his industry because the jobs of his subordinate managers were far too nebulous and, therefore, it would be impossible to set meaningful standards. When asked if there was any form of appraisal carried out in his company, he confessed that for the past 15 years annual appraisals had been carried out. The next question had to be: if there were no standards how had he appraised his people for the past 15 years? His reply was 'with great difficulty'.

Some of the difficulty experienced by managers stems from being confused by words which are in use in the vocabulary of management. For example, people often ask whether performance should be judged against goals, aims, targets or objectives, when in real terms the words mean the same thing.

18

Taking definitions from *The Collins English Dictionary*, one can see:

goal, *n.*   1. the aim or object towards which an endeavour is directed. 2. the terminal point of a journey or race.

aim, *n.*. . .   7. the object at which something is aimed; target. 8. intention; purpose.

target, *n.*. . .   3. a fixed goal or objective . . .

objective, *n.*   7. the object of one's endeavours; goal; aim.

For the sake of uniformity it would seem sensible to concentrate on objectives, as most managers do accept their use as an indication of what has to be achieved.

In general, people do feel comfortable being judged against the achievement of objectives, provided that the conditions and prevailing circumstances have been taken into consideration. However, judging people's performance only by the extent to which they achieve their objectives can occur too late as far as the company is concerned.

Take for example a manager of a football club. At the start of a game the objective could be stated as: to beat the opposition. The manager will not know until the final whistle whether the objective has been achieved or not. If it has not been achieved, there is nothing that can be done to change the result of that game.

It would be more productive to monitor the performance of the players during the match, comparing this with previously agreed standards of performance in the application of their skills. The previously agreed standard of performance for those players who are mainly employed to score goals could be expressed as: on target 7 times out of 10. The goalkeeper's standard of performance with regard to preventing the opposition from scoring could be: 6 shots out of 10 should be saved by totally controlling the ball in the arms, and an allowance of 4 shots out of 10 where the ball is only punched clear.

If all members of the team have standards of performance set against the main skills they are paid to apply, the maintenance or improvement of these standards will increase the chances for the team to achieve its objective which is to beat the opposition. Surely this applies to all businesses.

To improve performance, therefore, concentration must be towards the setting of standards of performance against the skills and activities required to be applied and carried out, in order that objectives may be achieved.

To develop practical guidelines for the understanding and application of standards of performance related to specific objectives, it will be helpful to approach the subject in three stages:

Stage 1 Where to set objectives and standards which indicate correct performance in the job of a manager.

Stage 2 The principles which should be adhered to if real commitment to the required standards is to be achieved.

Stage 3 How to set standards which are defined to the extent that the total job can be carried out to the highest performance level possible.

Stage 1 Where to set objectives and standards

An important decision, and one which requires considerable thought, is agreement on the objectives which each manager has to achieve, before time is spent determining standards of performance.

The main reason why time has to be invested here is the need for each manager's objectives to be contributing to the divisional/ company objectives, without being in conflict with any other manager's objectives.

There are too many instances where managers move into action towards the achievement of divisional objectives, without realizing how their actions can actually cause problems for other divisions—for example, the sales manager who embarks on a high-profile sales drive before checking with manufacturing and its related services to see how they could cope with an increase in demand.

To reduce this time waste, and resultant frustration, people must be working towards objectives which collectively contribute to the achievement of the company's main objectives. The responsibility to ensure that this happens is in the hands of all the managers within the company. This responsibility involves:

- double-checking to ensure compatibility of divisional objectives with the objectives of other divisions;
- looking closely at the total requirements of the positions within the division, and the tasks which people will have to carry out if the objectives are to be achieved;
- setting standards of required performance against the key tasks within each position.

In general, the position of manager can be described as having five main areas, where the requirement is to produce results:

- finance
- supervision
- communication
- development of staff
- the specialism

These are often referred to as a manager's *main result areas*. Concentration on only one or two, to the detriment of the others, will lead to short-term and/or long-term problems.

Each of the main result areas will contain a number of tasks which the manager is responsible for carrying out; these are often referred to as a manager's *vital key tasks*. The word 'vital' should act as a reminder that concentration must be on the tasks which are essential to the accomplishment of given objectives. For example:

Finance may include the tasks of controlling costs, maintenance of budget, quality, quantity, efficiency, profitability or margins.

Supervision will be related to the team working for the manager and will be concerned with safety, morale, job security, discipline, working conditions, throughput of work, labour turnover and appraisal of staff.

Communication is normally concerned with areas of reporting progress, running meetings, keeping people informed, liaising with customers and/or other departments, or making presentations.

Development of staff relates to the development of people within their current job, and will be reflected in the quality of training provided, the extent to which delegation is working, and the extent of coverage which exists for the manager's position and other key jobs in the department.

Specialism relates specifically to the nature of the position being managed, e.g. sales, finance, information technology, manufacturing, research and development, retailing, buying, personnel or training.

As a manager's success will depend on the application of organizational and interpersonal skills, and the application of the specific skills needed to accomplish the vital key tasks, this is where standards of performance must be established.

Stage 2   The principles of successful standard setting

These principles of successful standard setting are straight-forward, but relate to four crucial component parts and not one should be overlooked. These are validity, agreement, realism and clear definition.

VALIDITY

This seems a strange and rather obvious principle to start with, but there are managers around who do waste their time demand-ing standards of performance which have no real bearing on results.

The most typical example that many people suffer from is the area of appearance standards. There are occasions where appear-ance standards can be linked quite easily to the results expected in the job. For example, in a face-to-face situation with customers, or potential customers, it is important to project the correct company image. On the other hand, there are many occasions when the standard of appearance has no effect whatsoever on results. These standards are often just different people's views on what is considered to be appropriate. In this case we may have to recognize that other people's standards are different from our own, and as long as they do not affect the results, it might be better to learn to live with them rather than impose our standards on others. This should not be confused with the lowering of stan-dards. It is to do with some people's apparent obsession with views regarding the credibility, or otherwise, of men who wear suede shoes, or grow beards, or wear brightly coloured shirts and ties, and with girls who come into the office in trousers.

Another classic example, which has an even greater effect on time being wasted, is the case where the standard of performance is subconsciously imposed on job holders by managers making it clear that they believe good performers to be the ones who stay latest in the office.

Concentration has to be given to results, therefore the standard of performance must be valid in terms of these results.

Acceptance of this principle is important, if we are to reduce some of the self-imposed frustration, which can also have the effect of increasing conflict and damaging working relationships.

AGREEMENT

Arriving at agreement will be easier if we have followed the first rule of ensuring validity.

To achieve full commitment to a performance standard, however, genuine involvement with the person who has to perform the task is essential. Standards which are imposed unilaterally are really invitations to the other party to look for reasons why the standard cannot possibly be achieved. On the other hand, genuine involvement which arrives at positive agreement will more likely cause the individual to overcome any ensuing difficulties.

As a starting-point for agreement standards, it is worth examining the subject from three different standpoints, the past, the present and the future.

First of all let us assume a fairly normal situation, for example, seeking agreement on a sales standard for a product which has been on sale for some time.

The past Look back over the previous sales period. What sales figures were achieved, and what were the circumstances under which the job was being carried out?

The present What is the present situation like? Is it different in any way to the conditions prevailing over the previous period? Have we changed anything that could have made things significantly easier or more difficult? Possibly a new product that adds benefit to the existing produce, or tends to act as a replacement for the existing product. Are there any national trends that could affect us—for example, the unemployment figures or the competitors' activities?

The future   Is there any legislation in the pipeline which could affect our sales, either positively or negatively? Is there any evidence of new suppliers making inroads into our market?

The conversation with the job holder can then carry on with, for example: 'Let us summarize: we exceeded the target we set last year by 5 per cent, the present situation looks very similar to last year, with the exception that you now have more experience in this product line, and the problems in manufacturing seem to have been ironed out. Looking ahead, things in general do not look as if they will change significantly, although there is talk of an upturn in our market. Our major competitor had a hard time last year, so no doubt there will be an advertising boost from there. Taking all this into consideration, what do you think we should aim for?'

A concern expressed by many managers at this stage relates to their reluctance to allow this freedom to their employees, in the belief that they will seek a standard which will be easy to achieve, and so make their life easier. This may be true where relationships between the two parties are not good. Where the relationship is at least a reasonable one, people tend to behave in entirely the opposite direction. Following genuine consultation and an open discussion, a job holder who is asked 'What do you think we should aim for?' is more likely to set a higher standard. We do not like to let ourselves down. Surely we can recall saying to ourselves 'Why did I say that? I've made my life harder than I need have done.' This point should be picked up under the next heading, that of realism, otherwise you may have an unrealistic standard which can cause problems.

So much for the normal situation when historical information exists; but what about when we start from scratch? This question is very often asked. It can be relevant when the company has not been keeping records on a task, or no form of appraisal exists, or something new is being carried out.

If we use the *new* task as the example, it should help in the case of the other two situations. For example, assume that the research and development department has completed its task of designing a new product which has not been produced in quantity before. The manufacturing superintendent has been asked to produce an estimate of an acceptable reject figure towards which the department's staff should work.

The past   If the product has not been produced before, no historical information can exist. The easy way out is to wait and see how it goes. A more positive approach would be to consider similarity to any product produced before and allow for differences, and seek from the staff involved their opinion as to what could give trouble.

The present   What about today's working conditions in relation to this product's manufacture, and the workforce's familiarity or otherwise with the manufacturing process? How well are the operators being trained in the new techniques? How do they feel about the product or its implementation?

The future   How confident do the research and development team feel about their design and their anticipated difficulties?

Like everything else in the business of managing people, if you are dealing with the new and unfamiliar, success will depend a great deal on your projected enthusiasm. But it is still worth the question to the staff, 'What do you think we should aim for?'

Provided that the staff are aware that no one is going to hit them over the head if they are wrong, there is a good chance of achieving a good standard and real cooperation to make the product work!

REALISM

The standard that is both valid and agreed is a long way down the road to success—but if it is not realistic it has just been an academic exercise. We must face the facts of life: everyone may strive for perfection, but it is just not possible to achieve this very often. It may sound fine to say that if people agree to a standard that is beyond them, there will always exist the challenge to conquer it. This is not a very realistic point of view for the majority of us, and is even less so in the day-to-day management of people.

Consider for a moment a world-class athlete training for next year's world championships. How motivated to succeed would the athlete be if the standard to train to was 'to take one minute off the current 1500 metres world record'? There may be a few people who would accept this as a challenge, but even so, beating the existing world record by ten seconds is failure in terms of the standard set. Surely a more positive approach would be to look at that individual's record of improvement over the past year, consider the standards being achieved by other competitors, look at the facilities available for training, and arrive at an agreed standard that is, for example, to take one second off the existing world record. This could be a challenge to our athlete but it would be realistic with the possibility of achieving or even bettering it.

The same thing can be said about zero complaints from customers or zero rejects from the production line, although there is yet another problem highlighted here. This approach totally removes the opportunity to do better than the standard set. Far better, surely, to set a standard which is an improvement on the existing one, provided it is practical and realistic in terms of other conditions.

27

Most safety officers would like to see zero reportable accidents and some do, for periods of time. However, if the company's record is 7 per cent in relation to the total workforce, and it has been this figure for the previous five years, and if nothing has significantly changed in the company regarding process or layout for example, why not set a standard to aim for at, say, 4 per cent?

To sum up on realism, it is important to remember, when standards of performance are being agreed, that both parties should aim for levels which are challenging but realistic. Standards that are too easily achieved will not have the important effect of extending the job holder. At the same time, impossibly high standards may be treated as unattainable, and the job holder may even feel demotivated. We should aim for a level which the job holder can *just* exceed. The difference between 'two points short of standard' and 'one point over standard' is only three points in absolute terms. But the difference is quite marked in the mind of the person doing the job.

CLEAR DEFINITION

To measure, assess or appraise performance effectively, valid yardsticks must exist. The absence of objective measures means that performance can only be judged subjectively with the attendant dangers of bias, prejudice, inconsistency and inaccuracy.

Subjective evaluation of performance can also lead to the manager and job holder holding different views that can lead to conflict when performance is being discussed. An example of this occurs if the manager says to the job holder, 'Oh, I think you are doing OK in this aspect of the job.' A person's reaction to that could quite easily be 'What do you mean just OK?'

I recall a young manager's account of being interviewed by his manager in what was supposed to be an appraisal interview. The senior manager's preparation for the interview had been to complete a 27-page document by ticking appropriate boxes which were against the most subjective areas possible.

Early in the 'interview' the senior manager came to the item marked 'Initiative'. The senior manager said that he had assessed the subordinate manager as average. The latter indicated that it seemed reasonable and the manager seemed to breathe a sigh of relief and started to go on to the next box. The interviewee politely interrupted his manager and asked if he could please have some help. He said that he would like to be better than average so could he please have advice on two points:

- On what basis was average decided?
- What advice could the manager provide in order that he could become better than average?

Twenty minutes later the senior manager was still saying that it was very difficult, when the subordinate manager exploded with 'Of course it's difficult if you don't have anything to measure it against, and another thing, I don't like being called average without evidence!' The rest of the interview was quite difficult for the senior manager, I'm sure.

Whenever possible, therefore, performance standards should be as objective as is practical, that is, capable of being observed and defined. Facts and figures leave no doubt or ambiguity about whether the standards have been achieved or not.

Standards may be agreed in terms of positive numbers, for example, the number of invoices processed, inspections completed, enquiries obtained, or meetings held.

Standards may also be agreed in terms of negative numbers, for example, a reduction in the number of complaints, late deliveries, absenteeism, labour turnover, units rejected, miles per call, or stock levels.

On some occasions it may be more appropriate to set specific values such as sales turnover, production values, added values, efficiency ratios, return on investment, profitability, scrap and waste.

Time deadlines may also be used, like 'All invoices to be dispatched by the fifth day of the new period', 'Enquiries acknowledged within 48 hours of receipt' or 'New price lists in the hands of representatives within 10 days of a price change decision'.

A great number of managers believe quite sincerely that the tasks of their people, or themselves for that matter, are just too difficult to measure. This belief can stem from several sources. Sometimes the difficulty is actually to do with the monitoring of performance and not really the setting of standards. In other words the concern is about knowing whether a performance level is being achieved rather than not knowing what the standard should be.

On other occasions the difficulty is more to do with individuals not being totally in control of their own performance, a reliance on other people from other departments doing their jobs properly being the main concern. This situation applies to all people to some extent. However, when the expected standard is being discussed, the conditions and circumstances under which the performance has to be achieved must be taken into consideration.

Another difficulty managers experience, when trying to agree standards of performance, comes from looking at the whole job as a global subject. For example, trying to agree a standard as to how well the person supervises or communicates will be difficult, therefore these global or nebulous areas have been separated out into the related tasks.

Sometimes the word 'difficulty' is used to cover up a fear of failure to achieve or maintain an agreed standard, resulting in blame being passed to the job holder when outside influences affected performance. Anyone who reports to a truly professional manager should not have any concerns here, as shortfalls in performance will be analysed for the real cause. It is the amateur manager who assumes the cause of a shortfall to be the sole responsibility of the job holder.

How to set standards of performance

Setting performance standards requires attention to be focused on effects or consequences which have to be produced or avoided, rather than on the task itself.

For example, the task might be the control of outstanding accounts, whereas the required standards of performance may be expressed as:

● contain the number of overdue accounts to no more than 15 at any one time; and
● total value of overdue accounts should not exceed £40,000 at any one time.

Using some or all of the following questions will help you to define relevant standards of performance. Individually each question may not provide the answer, but practice in the use of the questions can develop a discipline which will produce a clear definition of what is required.

RECOMMENDED QUESTIONS

● What is the effect you require?
● What is the effect you are trying to avoid?
● What is the consequence you wish to achieve?
● What is the consequence you need to avoid?
● Why is there a requirement for this task?
● Describe what you mean by performing properly.
● What is your objective in doing the task?

- What would happen if the task is performed badly?
- What would happen if the task is performed well?
- What would happen if the task is not performed at all?
- Why cause this to happen?
- Why enable this to take place?
- Why prevent this from occurring?
- Why provide this information?

Normally your questions will reveal a clear indication of what is required.

The following example demonstrates how relatively easy it can be to establish useful standards of performance, which assist the job holder in working towards improvement in performance.

During one of our training courses in a large pharmaceutical company, a lady mentioned that a part of her job included making presentations, and could we advise her how to establish reasonable standards of performance? Currently her manager would appraise her against her presentation techniques, but of course this meant that her manager had to attend the presentations, or at least have the presentation taped for analysis later.

The task therefore is making presentations, so what are the effects or consequences required as a result of the presentations? This is what we had to establish.

In trying to clarify her objective we asked why she was making the presentations. Unfortunately this was a poor question because her reply simply informed us that she had been told to by her manager.

It later turned out that this lady was making presentations to the sales force on new drugs which had recently been developed. The purpose of the presentation was to advise the salespeople regarding the features and benefits of the new drug in order that it could be sold to doctors.

A poor presentation would be unlikely to equip the sales force to sell the new drug at the predicted sales figures. This seemed to suggest that sales of the new product could be an indication of the lady's performance, although such an assessment would be quite unfair as there were too many other factors which could influence the success of a sale.

Stepping back to the effects which are more realistically in the control of the lady in question, it became clear that if she does not succeed in providing the information required during the presentation, the salespeople will have to call back for additional information. An ideal presentation with regard to the provision of new product information could therefore be described as one where the sales force has no need to call back for information.

One of the standards of performance could be described as the extent to which people have to make repeat calls for information which should have been provided during the presentation. There could also be standards of performance relating to the costs and timing of the presentation.

This practical approach to agreeing defined standards which contribute to the company's performance also provides opportunities for the person employed to carry out the tasks, to work with purpose, and to improve performance to an extent that can be recognized.

Table 2.1 gives examples of standards of performance developed for a sales manager by using the recommended questions. There may be examples in this table which will be immediately suitable for you in your managerial position. For the remainder of your job, and for the jobs of the people who report to you, follow the recommended questions—they will work for you. There is an exercise in Chapter 9 of this book, which provides the opportunity for you to practise the skills of standard setting.

On the occasion where you find that it is not possible to recognize effects or consequences regarding a specific task, you are either tackling an area which requires further separation, or

Table 2.1   Examples of standards of company performance

Vital key tasks	Standards of performance
Finance	
Budget maintenance	No greater than $+15\%$ variance
Quality costs	Returned products as a result of sales department error to specification, no greater than 5% total sales value
Labour costs	Within agreed labour budget $\pm5\%$
Profitability/margins	Profit margin on sales of special products to be maintained at $22\% \pm2\%$. Profit margins on all other sales to be maintained at $30\% \pm5\%$.
Supervision	
Selection of personnel	Vacancies created by unexpected leavers to be filled by suitable applicant(s) within 7 weeks. Vacancies created by planned leavers, i.e. promotion, to be filled by planned replacement with no more than one week gap.
Organization of the team	All areas to be able to be covered by a least one salesperson at any time. No unnecessary duplication of coverage at any time.
Appraisal of staff	All staff reporting to you to have agreed standards of performance for all vital key tasks, within 3 months of being in the position. Reports on the performance of all

Table 2.1 (*cont.*)

Vital key tasks	Standards of performance
	staff to be submitted to the district manager within 6 days of any previously agreed dates.
General discipline	All matters of general discipline to be dealt with by the sales manager. No more than 5% which require involvement of district manager/director.
Labour turnover	To be maintained between 20% and 25%.
Communication	
Reports	Monthly sales reports to be accepted by the district manager no later than 3 days from each month end. Any 'special' reports to be accepted by the district manager within 3 days of requested date.
Keeping people informed	All policy statements issued by the company, which are for the attention of your staff, to be communicated to your staff within 3 days of your receipt of the information. Decisions made by yourself which have an impact on the jobs/performance of your staff to be communicated to the staff within 3 days.
Making presentations	Achievement of objectives of

35

Table 2.1   Examples of standards of company performance (*cont.*)

Vital key tasks	*Standards of performance*
	presentations to be measured within an agreed time-scale. New product presentation to be made to customers within the agreed time-scale following the launch.
Staff development Training	Training needs analysis to be carried out on all staff at least 4 times per year. Needs identified to be catered for within the agreed time-scale. 'New' skills to be monitored to ensure correct application.
Training (new products)	As new products are introduced, the relevant staff to be trained in the required new skills within the agreed time-scale.
Coverage	All areas to have sufficient staff developed to cover for sickness in the Key Areas. 3 members of your staff should be developed to cover the key parts of your job in order that the function of sales management can continue in the event of your unexpected or planned absence.
Specialism Market penetration	Obtain increase of 7% on existing market share with special products.

Table 2.1   *(cont.)*

Vital key tasks	Standards of performance
	Gain 10% share of regular product market.
New products sold	Obtain 3000 units of 'new' products. Sold at standard unit price.
Profitability of new product	Gain at least 5% margin on all new products sold.
Sales presentations	Organize and run 5 sales presentations per year.
Sales margins	On total sales, the margin generated must not fall below 12%.
Maintenance of records	Customer records should never be more than 7 days out of date.

you are endeavouring to establish a standard of performance for a part of the job which does not warrant the effort.

This next example demonstrates not only the application of standard set questions, but also highlights the need for progress to be monitored regularly. The example is taken from a situation in an insurance company. A supervisor is in charge of a team which has to respond to a tremendous number of different types of queries over the telephone from customers and potential customers. As the supervisor explained, there is no way of knowing how many calls there will be in one day, or indeed the nature of each call. It is important that the company should know whether, in the eyes of the people phoning in, this team is providing a satisfactory service. But how can the supervisor possibly set a standard for the performance of the team? A very reasonable concern.

The supervisor was asked: 'What happens if the team do not handle the query to the customer's satisfaction?' She replied, 'They get passed on to me to deal with.' This, of course, did not provide the complete answer, but it did help her to focus on a measurable standard.

A standard could now be set at a reduction in the number of calls which have to be referred back to the supervisor.

Unfortunately information was not available regarding past or present performance levels, so the supervisor decided to start a simple monitoring procedure. By recording in a notebook the occasions when calls were referred to her, she collected information regarding the number of calls and the nature of calls which certain people could not handle.

After a few weeks the supervisor was able to take actions which were aimed at reducing the number of referred calls by 10 per cent, as an initial step.

By continuing to monitor the performance of each person, and feed the information back to the respective individuals, a standard of performance was established at 95 per cent of calls received to be handled by the job holder.

Acceptance of the realistic allowance for 5 per cent of the calls to be referred to the supervisor provided everyone in the team with a realistic performance level, and greatly reduced frustration which had previously existed in the team.

The company considered the actions taken by this supervisor to be a worthwhile investment, which would have the effect of improving customer satisfaction.

A CAUTIONARY NOTE

All of the guidelines, examples and tips contained in this book are intended to help managers and their companies to improve their performance. A result of this may be that the task of managing people will become easier, but managers will still be busy! The principle of setting standards of performance for all the vitally important tasks is without question correct, but there is no point in setting standards if the cost of monitoring the actual performance outweighs the return of the benefits in improved performance. Monitoring performance is just like any other aspect of management: it has to be effective, but it must be efficient—keep it simple.

Guidelines for setting performance standards

- Clearly identify the individual's main result areas; these may be, for example, finance, communication, staff development, supervision and the specialism.
- Select the vital key tasks, those priority tasks from the result areas which, when performed well, ensure that the required objectives are being achieved.
- Set standards of performance against each of the key tasks which, when met, are acceptable to all concerned. Use information from past experience, present conditions and any foreseeable future changes.
- Standards must be valid in terms of result in the job.
- Agreement between the job holder and the manager will work towards commitment and cooperation.
- Ensure that standards are realistic—and not too easy!—but present a challenge which is within the job holder's capability.
- Strive for a clear definition at all times; standards which can be defined clearly minimize doubt and ambiguity.
- Arrange for information regarding actual performance to be available, to allow for the appropriate recording or monitoring.

3.

Reviewing the record

The next step in the process of appraisal is to collect information which will allow an objective comparison of results with the standards previously set. There should not be too much difficulty in this area provided that objective standards have been agreed and information sources are available to provide relevant and accurate details of actual performance.

It seems fair to assume that most people would agree that judgements should not be made at this stage, although a great deal of evidence shows that certain prejudices do allow this to happen.

A manager described such a situation which does seem to be typical in effect, if not in detail. A subordinate manager was transferred to a new location and with the job was a company-owned house for the use of himself and his family. A minor snag in this arrangement was the fact that the house had a nest of ants in the foundations. Many attempts had been made previously to rid the house of these insects, but without any real success. Consequently, since his arrival, the new manager had made several requests to the company's personnel manager to the effect that, although he and his family were delighted with the house itself, would the company please do something to rid the house of this unwelcome hoard of guests.

The net result of all this was that whenever this manager was being appraised by his boss, whatever results had been achieved in the job, he was always looked on as the person with the ants problem. A less than satisfactory assessment always seemed to emerge!

The example demonstrates that, although a job may be done well, other factors totally outside the result areas can significantly cloud the issue.

My daughter revealed to me an example which is not a million miles from this tendency. During a reasonably hot summer's day she had kicked her shoes off under her desk. Her boss called her in in a hurry, so she dashed into his office minus her shoes. Nothing was said at the time but, when her performance was being discussed, reference to her walking about the office without shoes always seemed to take priority.

Overcoming this kind of error in emphasis can be very difficult for certain people, and other human frailties can add to the error rate.

There is the tendency to oversimplify things, when the information relating to the person's performance appears to be very complex and, therefore, will require a great deal of effort to be specific. It is much easier to take an overall view and say that things look all right. This view could be totally unfair to the individual concerned, or equally unfair to the company, if it is not shown precisely what results have been achieved.

There was an occasion in a data-processing department when one of the agreed standards for the project leader was that projects should be completed within 15 per cent of the estimated time-frame. This had been agreed as a reasonable standard of performance, considering the past performance and the complexity and differences in the various projects under way. However, when the time came to compare actual performance with the agreed standard, many changes had taken place on 2 of the

41

projects out of the 12 under her control. The appraising manager's view was that 'She's not far off target and she's had some difficulties, so I'll rate her as being OK.' On this company's rating scheme this meant that she would be rated as an average performer.

Fortunately, there was an intervention by the appraising manager's boss, who said that this overall assessment could be unfair to the project leader. The insistence on looking further into the situation did reveal that the handling of each of the changes with the resultant amendments to estimated completion times was well above all their expectations. Luckily for the project leader and for the company the appraising manager did not suffer from one of the other tendencies, that of rigidity, although there are many who, having made up their mind about someone, seem to stick to that decision even when a lot of evidence suggests that a change of mind is necessary.

Another tendency to be wary of is that of seeing people as stereotypes—the tendency to attribute to people the characteristics of the groups to which they belong. For example, seeing all people in finance as having the same strengths or weaknesses; or that all personnel staff behave in a typical way; fortunately for us all they rarely do!

These basic sources of error can lead to a job holder being overrated or underrated, depending upon the prejudice held.

Overrating people, or what is often referred to as the 'halo effect', can cause us to see only what is good, even to the extent of exaggerating a supposed strength and overlooking a weakness.

Underrating people, or the 'horns effect' does the opposite, overlooking any strength but concentrating on a supposed weakness, and often exaggerating this beyond belief.

Halo effect

Looking first at the halo effect brings in examples like the good performance in the past, causing us to overlook completely what is happening in the present situation. There was the case where the job holder had previously done an absolutely marvellous job, every target achieved within the constraints and no problems whatsoever, but things had changed. Performance over the last few months had dropped significantly but there was no way his boss would admit to it. 'Look at his record in the past' was the cry, and 'It's more difficult today.'

There is also the situation where compatibility can cause the halo effect. 'He agrees with my views so he must be right.' It is nice to find people who agree with us but there will be times when we both may be wrong. When we are guilty of failing to see what is actually being achieved because of a prejudice, it does no good to anyone. There are cases where the prejudice extends to attendance at the same school or university, or similar job experience in the past, and it can be quite difficult to dissociate yourself from these compatibilities, but it is essential that it is done.

The halo effect can also come about by attaching undue importance to events that happened recently. If someone has very recently done a particularly good job, or helped you out of an embarrassing situation, it is possible that a degree of rationalization will take place subconsciously to excuse the job holder from a less than satisfactory overall job performance.

Of course there are also cases where people can be blinded by someone having an outstanding asset that does not contribute to that person's efficiency in terms of real results. A conversation overheard at dinner one evening was an example of this. Two managers, employed by the same company, were discussing the performance of one of their staff. Apparently this company had an appraisal scheme that graded people between two extremes, like

43

'sinks under the first sign of pressure' at one end of the scale, to 'walks on water' at the other. The conversation between these two managers started by one of them stating that he had to appraise one of his staff the next day. Both of the managers knew the job holder in question, so things were openly discussed. The theme of the discussion at first was to the effect that appraising this person was really a waste of time. As supervisor of the mail room this individual was turning in some pathetic results. Mail ended up at the wrong location; when it did arrive at the correct place it was invariably late; and generally speaking the department was in a mess.

As the conversation went on it was noticeable that it was taking a different slant. One of the managers casually said that the job holder in question at least had a good sense of humour. As they continued to discuss the point it seemed that their previously held views were changing. 'He's a tremendous boost to the morale of the department', and 'When the complaints roll in he certainly knows how to pick up the staff and let them see the funny side of it' were typical of the statements which followed.

The result of this change in the conversation was that both of the managers appeared to consider this person to be an asset to the company; no doubt he ended up with a commendable appraisal the next day!

Horns effect

Looking at the opposing set of views where the tendency is to underrate people by what is often referred to as the horns effect, can also be quite revealing.

Some managers describe themselves as perfectionists, not by actually saying that they are perfect, but by demanding perfection from their staff. To these people any job holder providing less than perfect work will always be underrated. This must be a totally unfair way to view anyone's performance, as no one can be perfect all the time! Allowances must be made for slight imperfection. After all, we surely expect people to make allowances for our imperfections, so why not the same attitude towards others?

Non-conformity or self-comparison is another area where job holders can be underrated. This is not the case of someone refusing to conform to aspects of the company's standards, but simply doing things differently from the way the appraising manager sees as the correct way. An example which highlights this managerial attitude was observed during a discussion on the selection of a new foreman from a group which had been through some intensive training. One of the candidates had shown himself to be very successful in all aspects of the training programme. This included the classroom training sessions, practical training on the shop floor, and periods of assessment actually running a department.

When a vacancy for a foreman did occur, it seemed obvious that this particular candidate would be chosen, and he was. However, one of the superintendents who had been involved with the training and selection from the start added a strange statement: 'I agree with you all in every aspect of what has been covered, but I would not have him if the vacancy was in one of my departments.' When questioned on this apparently conflicting remark he replied, 'Have you not seen the way he walks?' Thinking we had made some ghastly mistake, we admitted that we had seen this person walking and that he appeared to manage the task quite well. The superintendent's reply to this was, 'Yes, but he just *walks* through the department. I like people who move fast!'

An even more deep-rooted prejudice, that can make it almost impossible to get a fair assessment, is that which comes from guilt by association. If someone has ever been associated with a resounding mistake or failure, it can be very difficult indeed ever

45

to erase this from the mind when looking at current performance.

A personal experience of this came some months after inheriting a department that did have room for improvement, though very little of this was due to the quality of the staff in the department. When discussing the progress of the department with my immediate manager, we also discussed the individual contribution made by each member of staff. At the mention of a particular person whom I had reported as doing a very good job, I was told by my manager that I had obviously misread the situation. My defence of this individual was halted with the declaration that I did not have all the facts, because three years before I took the department over, this individual had been part of a team which made a mess of a particular project.

I doubt whether my attempts to explain that there had been no recurrence of this situation, and that the standards of performance were being achieved by this individual, made any significant impression in the mind of the manager.

Although the next chapter deals with the analysis of differences between standard performance and actual performance, and, therefore, should eliminate many of the effects of our affinities and prejudices, there still has to be a determined effort by us all to minimize the number of occasions when measurement is allowed to be overruled by judgement.

For performance appraisal to be truly effective and likely to achieve its objective of improving performance, the review of the record must be based upon information which is:

- relevant to the performance standards previously agreed, for irrelevant information will cloud this issue;
- complete, in that the information should cover the *entire* period under review leaving no gaps;
- explicit, in that it will allow the person making the assessment accurately to determine both whether the agreed standards

have been met, and the true extent of any shortfall; and

- accurate, as distorted information will lead to distorted analysis. This will most likely result in an uncomfortable interview, which will fail to gain agreement on those follow-up actions which are in fact the most appropriate to remedy performance discrepancies.

Accuracy will only be possible when a truly objective analysis of the differences between desired performance and actual performance has been carried out. This is dealt with in Chapter 4.

A summary of human attributes of which to be wary

OUR PREJUDICES

Trivia   Allowing factors which have no bearing whatsoever on the results in the job to influence the interpretation of performance information. This includes some personality traits.

Oversimplification   Ignoring complicating factors in order to keep things simple.

Rigidity   Having made up your mind, wanting to stick to that decision although evidence says that a change of mind is necessary.

Stereotypes   The tendency to attribute erroneously to individuals the commonly attributed characteristics of the groups to which they belong.

EFFECTS OF OUR PREJUDICES

Basic sources of error can result in our seeing people as if they are wearing a halo or horns.

Halo effect   Overrating the individual's record of performance.

- A good past record: this can cause us to fail to see that things have changed for the worse.
- Compatibility: similar beliefs or background may not always be relevant to performance.
- Recency: events which are fresh in the mind can over-influence our thinking and erase previous poor performance.
- Outstanding assets: being outstandingly good at one thing may make us blind to other areas which are well below standard.

Horns effect   Underrating the individual's record of performance.

- Perfectionist manager: ruthlessly downgrading anyone who does not meet impossibly high standards.
- Non-conformity or self-comparison: seeing someone achieve results by different methods from yourself.
- Guilt by association: where a person has been associated with a resounding failure, it could influence the appraiser's assessment over a much longer period than it warrants.

Of course all the above are made even worse if you should allow omniscience to creep in:

'But I am the boss, so I must be correct!'

4.

Analysis of differences between desired and actual performance

The situation having been appraised, there should be a clear picture that shows up any discrepancy between the required and the actual performance. For many managers, unfortunately, this is the time to jump in and tell the job holder that an improvement is required. This is based on the familiar, misguided assumption that performance can be affected only by a deliberate lack of effort or the need for a training course. Both of these could be true, of course, but in by far the majority of cases they are nowhere near to the truth.

On one occasion when a manager was seeking advice for the improvement of one of his subordinate managers, an example of this came to light. The company ran an extremely sophisticated performance appraisal scheme of the Christmas tree variety: 'Now that we've got one let's hang as many things on it as we can.' It was fully documented and its many pages included promotability, next job in three years, salary, personal history, comments from other people worked for, a grading against some fairly objective criteria related to performance in the job, and many more subjective areas, plus the training that the individual should have. Because it contained all this information, the whole exercise had to be handled very confidentially. So confidentially, in fact, that staff were never allowed to see anything written about them.

The manager in question had been graded as having a less than satisfactory performance. No other comments about development plans, but one small statement which read, 'This man is very lazy.' Being called in to give advice and having no knowledge of anti-lazy training courses, I had to ask the question, 'What does he do to cause you to say he is lazy?'

'That's easy to answer,' replied the senior manager. 'Every time I give him a job to do, you can see his mind ticking over as to whom he is going to give the job, and I don't like that.'

I hinted that the individual might think that he was doing a good job of delegation, but the manager soon put that right.

'I don't want him to delegate as much of his work as he is doing. How will I know he can handle specific parts of his job that I want him to do himself?'

That certainly put me in my place, so I asked if the person knew which parts of the job he was supposed to do himself, and not to delegate to others.

The reply, 'Well, he ought to know', could not be argued with. After being told this several times using different words, I asked if he had ever told the man specifically; he admitted that he had not.

In case this example is seen as a rather obvious and ridiculous thing to overlook, let it be stressed that unfortunately it is not an isolated case; it occurs far too often.

It is only human occasionally to forget to explain fully to someone what is expected, and I'm sure we have all been guilty of this at some time or another, but there is a point of view which was put forward which disturbed me.

I had been asked by one of Britain's largest and possibly best known companies to address ten of the most senior managers on the subject of appraisal skills. To introduce the analysis step, I quoted the example above regarding the over-delegating manager. The most senior manager in the group of ten interrupted in a loud gruff voice with, 'Sack him,' to be followed immediately by nine equally gruff voices echoing 'Hear, hear.'

Being taken aback by the comment and the chorus, I asked them to tell me which person they thought should be sacked, and why. The reply came from the original speaker, 'Sack the subordinate manager, he is not using his initiative, don't you know.' Again there were nine voices in chorus with 'hear, hear.' More was yet to come; the most senior manager went on to inform me that the people who work for us should know what we are thinking.

The analysis of difference between desired and actual performance is nothing more sophisticated than a framework of questions which will minimize the number of occasions when we miss the obvious; it is straightforward but essential and is represented as a flow chart in Figure 4.1. Although it is integral to performance appraisal, the analysis can also stand on its own when dealing with anything which can loosely be described as a people problem.

Step 1   The description of the problem

Describe exactly what the person is doing or not doing at work to cause you to say you have a problem. The easy situations to recognize are when it can be said that '93 per cent efficiency is the standard, the actual is 87 per cent' or 'seven calls per day is the standard and the actual is five'. These factors will have been identified during the action covered in the previous chapter. However, judgements—like 'uncooperative', 'lazy', 'untidy', 'lacking in self-confidence', 'poor appearance'—may have been overlooked and must be spelled out to describe the action clearly.

For example, 'uncooperative' may be described as: 'Two years ago this person could be relied upon to help us out of a difficult situation, but now it's a case of doing only what is contained in the

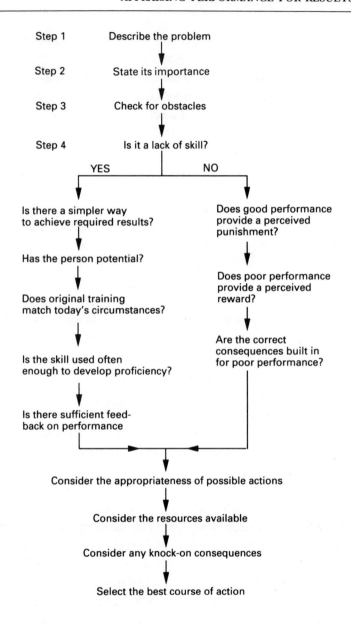

Figure 4.1   Analysing performance problems

job description', or 'Reports are regularly late, and have to be chased every month's end!'

I recall enquiring as to how a recently appointed salesman was performing. The sales manager said that he was not performing very well at all, his figures were down, and in fact it looked as if the new salesman would not be kept in the company for long.

My next questions were directed at finding out which part of the job the salesman was having difficulty with—for example was it to do with getting appointments? Was it to do with him not getting to see the correct person, i.e. the decision-maker or influencer? Was it the handling of objections? Or was it the closing of the sales? All of these questions were met with the admission that the sales manager had not thought about it like that!

In other words this sales manager was tackling the problem of poor sales figures, without being able to describe in precise terms what the salesman was doing or not doing to cause him to say he had a problem.

Step 2 Determine the importance of the problem

What must be done now is to determine the importance of the problem, in terms of results in the job. For example, what would be the result if it was left alone? Would the effort required to change the situation have any worthwhile effect on the job?

A situation that was described by the manager about one of his staff started out as the 'He is very untidy' case. The description of the problem was simply 'Papers are all over the place on his desk.' In trying to determine the importance of this concern, it was probed by questions like: 'Does he lose vital information? Could he be setting an example to the rest of your staff which they may copy? Do you find difficulty in locating information when this person is not at his desk? Does this infringe any confidentiality?'

All of these questions, and many more, revealed that nothing seemed to go wrong because of the lack of order. 'Why then, do you see this as a problem?' brought the reply, 'I just don't like it!' His colleagues who were present at the time said in chorus 'We've been telling you to forget it for the past five years, you've become neurotic about the chap.'

The message is simple. If the only result that can be identified is the way that the results are achieved, is it worth using energy, and the risk of upsetting people, trying to change anything?

It is almost as bad as the situation when a salesman with a fantastic record of success was criticized by the boss as being too quiet. 'Salespeople must have drive,' he said!

Sometimes of course, the way that people achieve results can be quite significant. An outspoken, brash, impatient go-getter can on occasions manage to succeed in running a department quite well. However, if there is a possibility that this person's approach to people could frighten off would-be applicants who had better skills, or could cause friction between departments, then the situation would have to be addressed.

Step 3   Do major obstacles exist?

Try to establish if any major obstacles exist, which are totally outside the person's control. These can be in areas like national trends, environmental conditions or even company-policy decisions that have inadvertently affected the situation since the standard was agreed—for example, an increase in unemployment in a salesperson's area, extreme weather conditions over a period, or even a tighter control on expenditure over the company as a whole, without the realization that a particular account would actually require more money to be spent for its existing standards to be achieved.

While the progress of a warehouse manager who had been

through one of our open training courses was being assessed, the following example emerged.

For many months prior to the manager attending the course, there had been a problem in the warehouse with one of the people employed to pick components from the shelves of the warehouse and pack the items for dispatch.

The person in question had been disciplined for carelessness to the extent that a final written warning had been issued. The carelessness was described as frequent inaccuracies in stock figures. The job involved the use of an electronic wand, which had to be passed over the bar-code on the components. This person was said to be careless while doing this because on occasions the information transmitted was inaccurate.

The manager admitted that after he had been on the course he looked at this situation by using the framework of questions. After describing the problem, and determining its importance, the question of obstacles to performance was raised.

The outcome of this revealed that the electronic wand which this person was using had an intermittent fault in it. On occasions it would misrepresent the figures it had to input.

The cause of the problem of inaccurate stock figures was resolved, but I don't know the extent to which the employee fully accepted an apology for the months of reprimands and disciplining.

Step 4   Is it a skill deficiency or not?

If the previous stage (Step 3) reveals that apparently no major obstacles exist, it is important now to establish whether the shortfall in performance is due to lack of skill or knowledge.

A very useful technique for establishing whether the present skills or knowledge are adequate for the desired performance is the answer to the question: 'Could people perform as desired if their lives actually depended on it?' A drastic question of course, but if the answer to the questions is 'No, if life depended on performance it would still not be possible', it would be fairly clear that the problem was related to a deficiency in either skill, knowledge or capability.

Assuming that the answer to this is 'Yes, it is a skill deficiency', and approximately 20 per cent of problems analysed this way do come into this category, let us follow the framework from there.

Is there a simpler way to achieve results?

It could be that there is a simpler way of achieving the results required. For example, changing the job by providing some kind of job aid, or storing required information on check-lists rather than relying on the memory.

At airports many years ago, it was possible to ask the check-in staff for information relating to interconnecting flights and this would be provided without much trouble. With the complexity of air travel today, it would be totally unfair to expect the staff to retain this information in their heads, so the details are stored and by pressing a button or two the answer is shown up on a visual display unit.

Does the person's potential match job requirements?

Jobs do change a great deal in many areas of industry and commerce. A person selected for a position some years ago may have had precisely the right potential to do the job at that time. In fairness to the individual, it is well worth rechecking to establish whether the physical or mental potential is there to cope with the job as it is today. It could be that the person is now over-qualified to do the job effectively or, of course, the opposite if technological advances have been made.

Does previous training match today's needs?

Having established that there does not appear to be a simpler way of achieving the results required, and that the person's potential does match with the job requirements, it is important that due consideration is given to the specific training that has been provided. Look at the training that was provided originally and compare this with the training that may be more applicable today. Again it is possible that the job has changed significantly, without the realization that different skills (technical, administrative or leadership) were being demanded. The chances are that the demands in one or all of these areas will change considerably over a period of time and it could be that the need to provide training has been overlooked.

How often is the skill required to be used?

It is possible, of course, that the job has not changed significantly and training of a formal nature is not, therefore, required. But looking at the frequency the skill is used may contain the answer to the problem.

Take, for example, a supervisor who is required to produce a budget forecast for the department. Initially the supervisor would be shown how to carry out an accurate forecast and complete the necessary paperwork. A standard will have been agreed relating to the accuracy and detail of the information required. If this supervisor only gets involved with this task once a year, it may be necessary to run a short reminder session each year as a budget preparation comes up. The use of the skills on a once-a-year basis is unlikely to provide sufficient practice.

Another example which can have a similar effect is the case of someone who is trained to do a job in readiness for a vacancy which may occur, for example when there is a need to have a stand-by person or as preparation for promotion. If the period of time between the provision of the training and the need for application is too long, it could be very difficult for the person to perform satisfactorily. A short refresher session would be more than useful in these cases.

What feedback on performance is provided?

At the other extreme, relating to frequency of use of the skill or knowledge, problems can occur by a very regular application. A group of women was trained in the identification of appearance faults on one of the company's products. One of the things they had to look out for was to recognize whether or not the company's logo on the product had been printed clearly. This was a difficult task, but the women developed a tremendous ability to do the job at speed while they were being trained and subsequently carried the job out on the production line. Everything went well for about six months and then customer complaints started to increase to a totally unacceptable level.

At this stage the company considered entering into a retraining programme to get the women back to the skill level required. But it was not a lack of training that was at fault. It had been assumed that a regular use of the skill would make the job easier to do, which, of course, can be true. What had been overlooked, however, was the fact that the women were comparing each day's work against the previous day's work instead of the standard which was approved at the start. The solution to that problem was the placing of an example to the approved standard on each work station—much less expensive than a retraining programme and with a much longer-lasting effect. However obvious this may seem, it is often the obvious that gets overlooked!

The previous example should act as a reminder for the need for feedback on performance. A phrase which may have caused us to forget this is 'practice makes perfect'. On its own this phrase is not true; practice can only make perfect when there is feedback on the performance. If people wish to improve their accuracy with a rifle, would there be much improvement if shots were fired blindly into the air? Of course not. A target would be aimed at and the feedback on performance would be the marks on the target.

The sadness of the situation is really seen when this extremely obvious example is totally forgotten in the business world. Two directors were discussing a new manager recently employed by their company. The conversation was basically an admission to themselves that they had made a mistake employing this particular person. 'I'm not happy about his appearance' and 'He's not producing the results we expected' were two of the comments made. A third party in this conversation asked if this message had ever been passed to the manager in question. 'Oh, he must know how we feel' was the reply.

The third party made a point of speaking to the new manager the next day, with a very low-key 'How are you getting on?'

'Fine thanks, settling in nicely, thank you!' was the reply. It was only when this manager was dismissed after four months' service that he knew to the contrary.

Apart from the human misery brought about by this lack of feedback at the correct time and in the correct manner, what a waste of potential which could have been harnessed and what a waste of money to the company's costs.

Feedback is essential where performance is concerned. If the performance is satisfactory, feedback will cause it to continue. If the performance is not as good as expected, feedback that is designed to be corrective can bring performance up to standard, bearing in mind that at this stage of the analysis it has been determined that performance is down through lack of skill or knowledge. Surely, it is obvious that feedback of the punitive variety can never succeed.

Taking this a stage further, what about the case when it is not a skill or knowledge deficiency? In other words the person could perform if life actually depended on it! It is not a training need but recognition of what is within the job, or the surroundings of the job, which could be determining the performance level. As stated earlier, 80 per cent of performance problems tend to be resolved by this part of the analysis and they do not often cost money in the resolution. That should show a saving on your training budget!

Does good performance result in a punishment?

It may seem a strange question to ask, but consideration has to be given to the possibility that performing as desired could be seen by the job holder as being geared to punishment. It does happen on occasions.

Promotion is sometimes stifled because of the difficulty in replacing a very good performer! But more often the punishment comes to the 'willing horse' with the resultant lack of willingness to help out. This comes to the surface as people being less than cooperative to the point of doing just what is paid for. Examples in this area are numerous. For instance, the job holder who helps out in the preparation of a very difficult report and, after many hours of very hard work, is greeted with 'Thanks very much, you've done an excellent job of that. I'll see to it you get more of these to do!' Unless that is what the job holder is looking for, more reports will be seen as a distinct punishment.

This approach may have very serious repercussions. On one occasion, when each individual manager had to be interviewed prior to some special training which was to be provided, all but one of the managers were available. The reason that one was not available was the fact that she was too busy to be interrupted. That is quite understandable, but to help out information was sought which would actually reduce the need to carry out the interview.

Reducing the need to interfere with the job being done at that time seemed to be the correct thing to do.

The information gained was briefly this: the unavailable manager was a young woman with tremendous ability and potential, whose qualifications fitted perfectly the company requirements. She was destined for a good career with the company but recently showed diminishing enthusiasm; she might be looking for a job elsewhere! Anxious to meet her, an enquiry was made as to what was the important task that prevented her from being interviewed. She was working out the monthly statistics! A job which she did every month occupying her for three days on each occasion. It was a job that a school leaver could do but this young manager made a superb job of it, so it was given to her to do every time, although it did not provide any challenge to her abilities, or any real interest. Is it any surprise that she was losing enthusiasm? (She subsequently left the company, but I doubt if her manager even really knew why.)

People are often expected to volunteer information to their managers, but what happens when they do?

In a medium-sized manufacturing company, a group of junior managers had been reminded that part of their duties included keeping senior management aware of any potential industrial-relations problems. Some weeks later, one of the junior managers reported a broken panel in an outside door which, if it was not replaced soon, could cause some problems with the operators as they were complaining about a draught.

The junior manager was told off for setting himself up as a spokesman for the workers—did he not want to carry on being a manager?

Often I come across examples where people are accused of being negative because they suggest better ways of doing things. This in many instances causes people to keep their mouths shut, and just to do as they are told.

Does poor performance result in a reward?

Providing punishment for good performance may seem to be a strange thing to do but what about actually rewarding people for doing a bad job? Take a look at the way that parents can do this with children. When a child is very untidy and leaves clothes around as they are discarded, a parent may just follow round and tidy up for the child! Or take the child who is described as having a bad memory; if it is raining in the morning the child will have to take an umbrella to school, and if it is not raining at going-home time the child may forget to bring the umbrella home. The next morning, if it is raining again, the parent will have to get the car out and give the child a lift to school. This can occur again and again and again.

The same thing can happen at work. If people are showing difficulty in handling particular tasks to the standard required, it can sometimes happen that managers will take the job away and give it to other people—or even do it themselves.

An example of this was seen in a team of financial auditors. The manager said that one of his auditors required training in the preparation of accurate and concise reports. The situation had developed over a period of twelve months.

When the manager took over the department twelve months previously he was not entirely satisfied with the way this individual wrote his reports. Instead of providing assistance to the individual in the form of explaining how to cover the points in question, the manager corrected the reports himself. This, as it turned out, had the effect of the auditor being less careful, because he knew that his manager would pick up and correct any mistakes.

The situation after ten months was so bad that the manager instructed the auditor just to provide a pencil draft which the manager could use to complete the report for the auditor. Perhaps the auditor was happy to get the job done for him!

Another example was observed in a small village office. One of the tasks of a woman in the office was to take the mail to the post office at the end of each working day. Apparently she discovered that if she left the office without the mail, the only consequence was that the manager of the office, who was usually last to leave, would take the mail himself. Not surprisingly, there was an increase in the number of times that the woman left the office without the mail!

Performance which is below standard can also be rewarded in two very different ways. The first is when a manager only actually speaks to a member of staff to provide a mild reprimand. Some people will specifically arrange for this to happen by doing something slightly wrong to get attention. It is, after all, recognition that the person is getting. Secondly, depending upon the seniority of the poor performer, the embarrassment of having such a performer in the company can sometimes have the effect of the individual being promoted out of the way. If this has even appeared to have happened in the past, it could be that others will try to follow.

One of the most obvious rewards for poor performance must surely be the case of the field engineer who was described by his manager as the slowest engineer he had ever employed. 'The quality of his work is good but he takes so long in his repairs, that we have to pay him $2\frac{1}{2}$ hours overtime every night to do his paperwork,' said his manager. The manager also informed us that he felt he had tried every way possible to speed up the engineer with his repairs. Ironically he had been doing just the opposite.

What actions are seen as a result of performance?

Taking this a stage further, it has to be established whether the performer can see a reason for the desired performance. In terms of the effort required to perform as desired, is it seen to be necessary in terms of results in the job? There are many different priorities within any particular job, and if the performer cannot see the need for a particular activity, then in that person's mind it will not be accepted as a priority. Take, for example, the need for salespeople to send in reports. Many sales managers complain about reports being late or that they contain insufficiently detailed information.

A sales manager decided on one occasion to get out on his own to visit some of his customers and was greeted on one such visit by 'I didn't think we did business with your company any more, it must be three months since we saw your salesman.' Being taken aback by this the sales manager telephoned his office to get extracts from the salesman's reports. Information from his secretary revealed that the last three attempts to visit the customer were aborted at the last minute by appointments being cancelled by the customer's buyer. When this message was relayed to the buyer in question, the reply was an apology for making the salesman's life difficult but on each occasion a very serious situation had occurred in the company; in future there would be a positive attempt to get a deputy to see the salesman if the buyer himself was unavailable.

Feeling very pleased now, the sales manager decided to mention this to all his salespeople at the next sales conference, which was due to be held soon. The message at the conference was going to be: 'The need for a report is not just to check up on you but also to protect you. That is why I need your reports to be in, and on time, and containing specific information.'

A fair point to put over, but why did it take three months and a visit to the customer to find out that the salesman was having difficulty? Instead of just filing the reports as they are received, why not some action to demonstrate that reports are actually used? The salesman's view of the situation could easily have been 'If the reports are only filed when I send them in, how can late filing be as important as making sales calls, for example?'

Another company was experiencing difficulty getting service engineers to complete their reports. This meant that invoices were late going out. The message had been communicated on many occasions to the service engineers that if invoices were late going out it would seriously affect the company's cash-flow situation. Some service engineers would respond to this and many may not have realized the seriousness of this state of affairs. Redesigning the paperwork involved making it more simple, and including in the new design the claim for the service engineer's personal expenses, could have a more lasting effect!

Many people search for ways to reward people if they perform well, and I suppose this is commendable. Some attention should also be paid, however, to providing an adverse condition where performance is down.

A district manager in the freight business was telling me about one of his depot managers whose time-keeping was a disgrace. Apparently he would arrive in the depot some time between 8.00 a.m., which was the official opening time for the depot, and 10.30 a.m. It was more often closer to 10.00 a.m. than 8.00 a.m. The district manager explained how he had spoken to his manager about the situation on many occasions, but no improvement was forthcoming. There were no extenuating circumstances, other than the fact that when this person was at work, the quality of work was good. The only other factor to emerge was the difficulty of finding suitable staff in this district due to the employment situation. In other words, 'He knows I would not be able to replace him' was the phrase used by the district manager.

A simple solution was accepted by the district manager, namely, to involve the depot manager in the design and detail of an advertisement which would be placed in the local newspaper.

65

The advertisement would read 'New depot manager required urgently'. As soon as the depot manager realized that his boss was serious about the situation, performance improved immediately.

Have other obstacles been built into the job?

It is always possible, of course, that obstacles have been built into the job which prevent, or at least make very difficult, the desired performance. These can be in the areas of lack of clarity of what or when something is expected to be done, conflicting demands on time, lack of authority, restrictive practices, or noise distractions from others.

An example in the area of distraction was observed when small teams of engineers were located in one office. Their main functions were in the design of new products, each team working on a different technical aspect of a product. They were located together to make it easy to interchange ideas and link in on design problems. As their need to contact people outside their office was minimal, only one telephone was installed. Initially this was to everyone's agreement and no problems were encountered.

After a period of time, complaints about lack of cooperation between the sections emerged. This escalated to complaints from other departments about the difficulty in being able to contact people in any of the sections. 'No one bothers to answer the telephone' was one of the regular complaints made.

The one telephone was sufficient to cater for the need for outgoing calls, but the problem related to incoming calls over the question of 'Who is it for this time?' Having to answer the telephone to find that it was for one of the other sections was having a twofold effect. First, the irritation of being disturbed unnecessarily led to friction between the sections; secondly, a case of letting it ring became the norm because it might be for someone in the other sections. Providing a telephone for each section soon proved to be a small investment when compared with the resultant improved performance all round.

In the search for obstacles which may be causing performance to be less than satisfactory, it is also necessary to look at the way that people are being managed. The overall attitude of the manager has a real influence on people's performance, much more than is often realized. Being approachable will encourage your staff to discuss problems with you before it is too late. Not allowing prejudices to influence relationships will enhance confidence and being sensitive with regard to others will provide advance warning of problems which could develop. Many conflict situations arise from these areas. It does seem to be true that good managers have good staff and what are described as bad staff tend to have bad managers. Very few exceptions to this rule exist!

Verification and actions?

Spending some time analysing the situation as objectively as possible will provide an answer, or at least a number of possible solutions, with regard to the performance discrepancy. A decision is now required as to the most appropriate action to resolve the situation.

Bear in mind that the job holder in question will have to be involved in discussions to verify what is thought to be the real cause of any shortfall in performance. This discussion will be much easier to handle if it is seen that the situation has been examined objectively. More information may come to light but at least you have demonstrated that you have not just made the assumption that more effort is needed.

In preparation for this discussion it will be useful to consider the possible solutions with reference to their appropriateness, or difficulty in implementation. The resources required will also have to be considered against the potential benefits. It is also

APPRAISING PERFORMANCE FOR RESULTS

possible, of course, that some solutions could cause problems in other areas. Consideration of these factors before the interview will make it easier to arrive at the best balanced course of action. Not only are you proving that you are following the good rule of being prepared but also that you consider the job holder important enough to invest some time to try to help.

Your own performance as a manager is being appraised by someone and one area could be your control of your budget. The analysis described will also assist you here by ensuring that you spend money only on training when it is actually the solution to the problem. Money is often wasted on performance problems by starting with the premise that training is the solution to all problems. Not only is this critical in itself, but also the more objectively performance is analysed, the greater is the chance to improve everyone's performance. And, after all, you are judged as a manager by the results achieved by your staff.

The analysis in summary

To establish the most likely cause of differences between desired and actual performance:

- accurately describe the problem;
- determine its importance in terms of results in the job;
- if the importance is significant in terms of results, check to see if obstacles outside the job have arisen which could be affecting the results required;
- establish whether the shortfall in performance is due to a lack of skill or capability, or the existence of other factors.

Should the answer be that the discrepancy is being caused by a lack of competence, consider:

- Is there a simpler way of achieving desired results?
- Does the person's potential match the job requirements?

68

- Does the training originally provided match the requirements of today?
- Does the individual utilize the skill often enough to develop proficiency?
- Is sufficient feedback on performance provided?

If it is thought that the person's competence is correct for the requirements of the job, and the cause of shortfall could be to do with other factors, look for evidence of:

- performing as desired providing a punishment in the eyes of the job holder;
- not performing as desired providing a reward to the job holder;
- a lack of action if required performance is not met;
- obstacles to performance which may have been built into the job.

Make a note of all aspects where verification is required when you meet the employee, and consider possible actions which could resolve the situation, should your analysis be correct.

5.

Preparing for an appraisal interview

Discussions with many managers on the subject of performance appraisal reveal that of all the skills which are necessary for effective appraisal, it is the actual face-to-face situation with the job holder that causes anxiety. Typical concerns are stated as:

- 'How can I possibly sit down and feel comfortable while telling someone that an improvement is needed?'
- 'No one likes to be told that he or she is doing a bad job, so how can I overcome or control the negative attitude which must emerge?'
- 'It is all right if I have good news to tell them.'
- 'What happens when I have to say that there is no salary increase?'

The common fault with all of these cases is that they are based upon the traditionally held view of appraisal, which regards appraisal as a one-way method of control and the interview is used solely for the purpose of informing the individual how well, in the opinion of the appraising manager, he or she has performed. This is not an interview and it will contribute very little towards effective performance appraisal, as it leaves out any input from the job holder.

The real objective of an appraisal interview must be: 'To

establish the true cause(s) of problems which are affecting the job holder's performance, and to develop a plan of action which, when implemented, will remove the cause(s), or at least minimize the effect on job results.'

For the full potential of performance appraisal to be realized the interview must, as the word implies, be an interchange of views geared to the problem-solving and planning process involving useful two-way communication. When this definition is accepted it becomes obvious that the concerns listed previously need not exist. For example, if you are genuinely interested in verifying the true cause of any shortfall in performance, your starting point will not be to tell someone that an improvement is needed. The chances are that the job holder will already be aware of this and might just appreciate the opportunity to contribute towards the resolution of the problem—a point which is more readily accepted when you put yourself in the position of the job holder.

The concern regarding the 'no salary increase' is a much more controversial subject. There are many opposing views regarding the link between appraisals and salary, although it would appear to be correct for some connection to exist where it is possible to provide extra money for performance which is greater than the agreed standard.

Even when there is agreement on this point, however, there is still considerable disagreement regarding the inclusion or otherwise of any discussion on salary adjustment during the appraisal interview itself. This must surely be resolved by the agreement that it is not possible to determine accurately any related salary changes until the true situation is clarified. This can only be accomplished fairly by listening to the job holder's input during the interview, possibly by further verification after the interview, and also by reviewing the situation with your own manager who will wish to see fairness all round.

After all, if during the interview, you tell your people that you are interested in their output, how can you possibly make your mind up firmly on anything before the interview has started? If you do, it is likely that your job holder would see the interview as a complete waste of time.

The rule should be to discuss salary at a separate interview some time later, and it will be in everyone's interest to ensure that all people working for you understand the reason for this decision. There will then be less likelihood for the subject to come up during the interview which will allow you to focus clearly on the real objective to be achieved. Clearly taking time out to sit down with your people will guide you to success and remove a lot of the reason for anxiety.

Lord Baden-Powell gave the world the watchword 'Be prepared'. It is a philosophy that applies in all walks of life and certainly loses no significance where performance appraisal interviews are concerned. Of course all interviews require preparation, but in the case of appraisal the actual preparation is quite different.

The good appraising manager starts the preparation for the interview as soon as the actual performance is compared with the standard of performance required. Notes will be made highlighting any significant differences, whether positive or negative, as these are the areas where analysis and discussion will be needed.

Reasons for highlighting the positive areas are threefold: first, it will be good to show that you are aware of and pleased with performance which is better than anticipated; second, if you can establish how the person achieved such good results it may show you how others could improve by a similar approach; and third, and this is an aspect with potentially more serious implications, it could be that better than standard performance in one part of the job is actually responsible for a shortfall in performance in another related area, for example, savings on a safety budget versus increase in accident rate, or an increase in call rate versus a decrease in actual sales.

The analysis of differences between desired and actual performance will also form a very great part of preparation. Apart from demonstrating the willingness and the skill to recognize that individuals are not completely in control of their performance, it will provide you, as the appraising manager, with information relating to what appear to be causes of differences in performance against the requirements in the job. This is a vital part of the preparation as these are the areas which require verification.

Preparation of the job holder is equally important. Typically that person may view the prospect of an appraisal interview with considerable trepidation, the extent of which will be largely determined by the relationship which exists between the appraising manager and the job holder. Do not be misled by the often-held assumption that job holders view the relationship in the same way as the manager supposes it to be. Make every effort to ensure that each of your people knows that the interview is going to be an objective exchange of views with a common purpose, which is performance improvement. Only those who see themselves as perfect could disagree with this as being a reasonable objective, and they would require a special interview!

A useful technique for job-holder preparation is to ask the individual two or three weeks ahead to go over his or her performance against the previously agreed standards, and to make notes against any of the result areas, both positive and negative. Ask the job holder also to note down any particular problems he or she would like to discuss which could be affecting performance.

Provided that your people know that you are going to listen, and it is not going to be one of those head-hitting exercises, their attitude towards the interview is likely to be very positive, which in itself is a very worthwhile part of preparation.

An example of a form which can be useful in helping a job holder to prepare for an annual appraisal is shown in Appendix 1.

With regard to the practical aspect of preparation, there are four very important rules which should not be broken.

Rule 1 The time and date for the interview must be firm. Only in the most exceptional circumstances can this rule be broken.

It is a real insult to your employee to say that the time or date for the interview has to be changed. By implication you are saying to the person in question that he or she is less than important.

Rule 2 The time and date for the interview should be set far enough in advance to allow adequate preparation by both parties, but not so far in advance that circumstances have an increased likelihood of changing. Consideration must also be given to the other person's schedule of work. As a rule of thumb, ten calendar days' notice seems to work for the majority of people. This is based on views that less than seven days is insufficient time for real preparation, and more than fourteen days increase the chance of having to reschedule.

Rule 3 Sufficient time should be set aside, and this communicated to the employee, so that the interview can be completed without interruption.

As a rough guideline, it is unlikely that an effective appraisal interview could be completed in less than half an hour, but on the other hand an interview lasting two hours could be rather awesome.

You know what you want to cover in the interview, but you do not yet know what it is your job holder may wish to cover, and yet your time planning requires you to make a decision about how much time to put aside. You will not want to be constantly looking at your watch, and you certainly will not want to have to close the

74

interview through a shortage of time as both of these could be distinctly counter-productive.

The best approach is to allocate about twice as much time as you think you require. This way you will be able to relax from the pressure and end the interview when the objective has been achieved. Should this happen well inside your allocated time you will always find plenty to do in the time you have saved!

Of course it is always possible that the opposite to this could occur. Your job holder may disclose a concern which you are not prepared for and the time required to do justice to it would take you well over the time you had allocated. In this case it could be worth agreeing to meet again in two or three days' time to complete the interview. When this happens, ensure that the time in between is used to collect and verify any additional information required.

Rule 4   The interview should be held in private with no interruptions. It does not impress your employee to see how many telephone calls you take, and thereby how important you are! Not only that, you should be demonstrating your managerial skills and this will be difficult if you are seen to be indispensable and unable to delegate.

Consider also the message the job holders receive when once in a while they are shown to be your most important concern. You will be communicating to your employees your positive attitude towards appraisal which will develop loyalty, and it will spread.

The application of all of the four rules presents additional difficulties to some managers, especially when they do not have their own private office, or a means to control incoming telephone calls and messages. This is most often experienced when the company is an open-plan environment, or the manager spends most of the time 'on the road'.

However, appraisal interviewing is not the only occasion when privacy and freedom from interruptions are essential. There must be times when you wish to work with someone on a new design, a new product, a new marketing strategy, or a confidential financial report. Therefore, the difficulties already exist and ways have to be found to overcome them; for example, arranging to use someone else's office, because even in the open-plan situation someone seems to have an office, or ensuring that an interview room is made available. The return on this investment of your time will more than compensate for the apparent inconvenience, particularly when the arrangements for appraisal interviewing are exactly the same as those other instances when privacy is needed.

There are some managers who believe that taking out the job holder for a drink is the best way to handle particularly awkward people. Apart from the ethics of this approach, it is difficult to imagine any real benefits emerging in the way of improved performance. It does not necessarily put the individual at ease, and very seldom does privacy exist. Furthermore where does it stop? If you take the person out for a drink to say that an improvement is needed, do you take him or her out for a drink when the improvement is achieved?

I recall a particularly nervous manager saying that he was dreading his appraisal interview because his boss had suggested that they meet for a drink to discuss his performance. 'I must be in for a real roasting if he's prepared to buy me a drink' was his cry. Of course it is always possible that getting a drink out of the boss is worth causing a bit of aggravation!

Questions are often asked regarding the most appropriate seating for an appraisal interview. The answer must be for you to do what you see as appropriate with each individual who reports to you; there can be no more of a hard and fast rule than this. Knowing your people will obviously help you to make this decision; however, as said previously, the smaller the number of changes you introduce into this part of the job, the better it will be for all concerned. For example, if it is your normal style to talk to your people while you are sitting behind your desk with the job holder sitting opposite, then that can be the most appropriate way to conduct the interview. Or if you normally discuss work around the table, or sitting side by side, then that will be the most appropriate seating for the appraisal interview. The point is that the desk, or the absence of the desk, can be a barrier between you if it is not your normal approach.

The first few moments of the interview are crucial in setting the tone of the meeting. The words used can have a lasting effect in determining whether cooperation is going to be uppermost in the mind of the interviewee.

Because these first words are so vital, sufficient consideration must be given to them when preparing the interview. It is too easy to overlook their importance and decide to play it by ear. The trouble with this is that when you are writing something out as part of the preparation, you have the opportunity to erase words or phrases you did not mean to use. When speaking you do not have this luxury. Words used and then retracted can remain in the mind of the receiver. For example, if you are feeling a little nervous it could be that your opening remarks to the job holder will accidentally portray a lack of commitment towards the time being invested in an interview. Phrases like 'Good morning, come in, I'm sorry to take you away from your work but we have these appraisals to do' cannot be fully retracted, however many times you say you did not mean it. A phrase used recently referred to the 'appraisal lark', though fortunately this was during a practice role-play situation!

It can be even worse to start off by confirming in the mind of the job holder that you pay only lip service to courtesy and politeness. This is done all too frequently by spending the first few minutes of the interview apparently enquiring into the health of the person's family, to be followed immediately with 'Well, sit down, we need to talk about your performance', irrespective of the answers the person gave.

It may seem insincere to suggest that you should prepare a courteous 'Good morning, is everything still all right with you for our meeting?' but it will pay dividends to be prepared for the answers you may receive. Should the answer be positive, you can then follow up with a reminder of the objectives of the meeting and go straight into your prepared framework. On the other hand, should the answer suggest that the situation has changed seriously and it is not really the best time to continue, offering to reconvene at a later date could be the best thing to do. Your offer will more than likely be declined but you will be showing under-standing towards the job holder and the importance of that person's role in the interview.

As part of your preparation sufficient emphasis must, there-fore, be placed on ensuring that your opening remarks and your whole attitude will be geared to emphasizing the positive and forward-looking aspects of appraisal and at the same time making it clear that both yourself, as the appraising manager, and the interviewee, as the job holder, will have an equal share in the entire process.

Thought must also be given to how you wish to cover the points highlighted for discussion. It is unlikely that you will know for certain what it is that your job holder wishes to bring up, but this must not cause you to neglect your preparation. It is always possible to prepare a framework which you would like to follow provided that it has an in-built flexibility to cope with the job holder's input.

When preparing the framework, consideration will have to be given to the specific individual in question regarding the number of occasions this person has been through an appraisal interview with you, the kind of relationship you have with this person, the number of points that you have for discussion, and your confidence in relation to the accuracy of your analysis of any difference between desired and actual performance. Depending on these variables, you can now consider the most appropriate sequence for the order of discussion, which will cover the topics in as logical an order as possible in relation to the functions within the job, but at the same time ensuring that the positive and negative attainments are reasonably mixed to avoid overemphasis on either side.

The final stage of preparation can now be covered and that is the preparation of the notes you wish to use during the interview.

It would be totally unfair to yourself and to your staff if you were now to rely on your memory after all the work you have put in. It really is amazing how easy it is to forget the most obvious and significant points. On the other hand, it could be very off-putting to arrive at the interview with a large pile of official-looking documents.

Short, succinct notes on the major differences with some analysis points and possible solutions will be much more appropriate. You can always have the back-up information to hand in case it is required.

A checklist for preparation

- Compare actual performance with previously agreed standards.
- List major differences.
- Analyse differences for possible causes.
- Consider possible solutions/actions.
- Advise job holder to review own performance against previously agreed standards.
- Agree firm time and date for interview.
- Ensure sufficient time is available for the interview.
- Arrange for privacy with no interruptions.

- Develop a framework and anticipated sequence for the interview.
- Prepare notes for use in the interview.

6.

Conducting the interview

The very manner in which an appraisal interview is conducted can determine and control the outcome. Many people experienced at interviewing agree that the appraisal interview can be one of the most satisfying and rewarding experiences a manager can meet, provided it is conducted properly.

A prerequisite of proper conduct is the recognition and acceptance of the fact that stress can play its part in destroying a well-prepared interview. Although it is quite natural for both the interviewer and the interviewee to feel under some stress before the interview commences, this stress must be controlled and its effect on the interview minimized if any useful interchange of views is to take place.

Looking first at the interviewer, it is possible to identify the most likely cause of stress, its effect, and possible solutions.

With the exception of a total lack of preparation, the most frequent cause of stress to managers is a lack of skill and experience in conducting successful appraisal interviews. Any feelings of inadequacy which this can cause will increase the stress, make the interviewer feel less than comfortable, and more than likely produce a resultant behaviour which will certainly not be conducive to the achievement of the stated objectives.

A conscious effort to improve is essential, and the more you work towards minimizing the stress on yourself the easier and more successful the interviews will become.

Practice at interviewing will lead to improvement, provided you receive sufficient feedback on your performance. It is very unlikely however that you will get real feedback from your employees, or if you do it is unlikely you will want to accept it!

This book is intended to provide the guidelines but it cannot develop the skill for you, neither can it give you a real insight into where there is a need for you to improve. This can best be done by practice interviews in front of a qualified trainer and by carrying out 'role play' interviews which can be recorded on video tape. You will then be able to witness the replay of the tape under the trainer's guidance, where you will see what you are doing well, and which areas need to be improved.

Depending upon the amount, and the quality, of the training you receive and the number of actual interviews you have to conduct, it is also recommended that you use a colleague to practise with as often as is necessary. Ideally these practice interviews too should be recorded on video tape. Although it may not always be a pleasant experience it certainly provides an excellent opportunity for improvement to be seen—an approach which is surely better than practising on your staff.

Should any of your employees be aware of the training you are receiving, and the practice you are going through, you will once again be demonstrating your positive attitude towards appraisal, which can enhance the respect they have for you.

Turning our attention to the interviewee, we find that there are a number of factors which contribute to his or her feeling of stress during the interview. First, and unquestionably the most important, is the relationship that exists between the manager and the job holder. The closer and more open the relationship, the less the likelihood that any stress will be experienced.

The frequency at which the manager discusses performance

with the job holder will also play its part. The more often there is discussion, the less will be the need to feel under stress, and the fewer occasions that performance is discussed the more likely it will be for fear to creep in, which in turn will increase the stress felt by the employee.

During the interview itself there are other factors which can increase the stress felt by the interviewee to the detriment of the achievement of the real objective. The most significant is known as 'power difference'. That is the power the interviewer has over the interviewee by the nature of the difference in structural positions within the company.

Actions by the interviewer must be aimed at reducing the effect of this difference in power in order that a good objective exchange of views is achieved. Actions and attitudes which do not reduce the effect of the difference will increase the stress felt by the interviewee and reduce the chance of the true attainment of the interview objectives.

It must be emphasized that should the interviewer be more than one level above that of the interviewee or, as in some organizations, the interviewee be faced with a panel of interviewers, the difficulty in reducing the effect of the power difference will be considerably greater.

With these thoughts in mind, we can now concentrate on ensuring that the interview becomes alive and resembles a smooth conversation; remembering always that the interviewee has to have the opportunity to do most of the talking in order that the true causes of performance are established.

Should you have any doubts about the real benefits in getting the interviewee to do most of the talking, or indeed whether that person will feel comfortable in this role, consider the last time you said you had enjoyed a conversation with someone. It is most likely you would comment on how much you had enjoyed talking to the other person, as opposed to listening! If we can get the job holder to feel this way we will be on the correct route to conduct good productive interviews.

The achievement of rapport, which will cause the interviewee to feel comfortable and willing to express genuine views, is reliant upon your skill in selecting and phrasing the appropriate statements and questions.

The use of statements in an interview should be restricted if the interviewee is to do most of the talking, but of course there are occasions when statements are necessary. For example, you may wish to start the interview by restating the objective, explaining how you would like the points developed, how you need the interviewee's input, and how essential it is that the interview closes with an agreed plan of action. In other words, your statements will be 'signposts' which will help you both to know the route you wish to follow.

During the interview itself statements will also be required, either to point the interviewee in the direction of your next question, or to bring the interview back on the correct road should it be digressing into areas which are not appropriate to this interview.

Using signposts at the required place is a very helpful technique to control the interview, but questions are even more important if the real objective is to be achieved.

The use of questions

The kinds of questions which require skilful use are those necessitating the interviewee to think and to talk openly without feeling under pressure. One type of question that does this is called the 'open' question.

EXAMPLES OF OPEN QUESTIONS

- 'To what extent does this . . . . ?'
- 'What importance does this have in relation to . . . . ?'
- 'Explain to me how . . . . ?'
- 'Tell me about . . . . ?'
- 'Describe to me how . . . . ?'

Another benefit of the open question stems from the fact that normally the response to the question will take longer to say than the question itself. This enables you to concentrate on listening carefully to what is being said. Sometimes the reply to the question may not be entirely clear, or you may feel that there is something under the surface which could be useful for you to know. To make sure that you understand what is being felt but not said, it could be useful to 'probe' a little deeper into the subject.

EXAMPLES OF PROBE QUESTIONS

- 'Better in what way?'
- 'Why do you think . . . ?'
- 'Oh?' or 'yes?'

Silence can also be used to collect more information. When the interviewee says something to you, it is normal that you would acknowledge the statement in one way or another. Should you fail to respond at all, your silence may encourage the other person to fill the gap in the conversation by the addition of more information; however, like any other technique, this should not be over-used or it will have an inhibiting effect on the interviewee.

To ensure that the interview is not seen to be jumping from subject to subject, it is useful to identify something said by the interviewee which will allow you to 'link' up with a topic you wish to pursue.

EXAMPLES OF LINK QUESTIONS

- 'You mentioned that it is difficult to find the time for all that has to be done. What are your views on delegation?'
- 'You mentioned your dislike for financial controls. How do you see our being able to improve the way that money is available for new projects?'

CLOSED QUESTIONS

Normally it is advisable to avoid the use of 'closed' questions which can be answered by a 'yes' or 'no' response, and there are good reasons for this. First, there is the difficulty of being sure that the response is really true; second, you are not getting the interviewee to initiate discussions or volunteer information; and third, you will increase the pressure on yourself by having to do most of the talking and thinking up a great number of questions at the same time.

However, there are those instances during an interview where this closed question can be most appropriate. At the start of the interview, while you are settling down the interviewee by collecting some primary facts, it can be quite acceptable. Another occasion when the closed question is appropriate is when you have been successful in getting interviewees talking . . . and they don't seem to want to stop! A quick closed question, slipped into a pause for breath, can work here. The third occasion closed questions are appropriate is at the end of the interview, to summarize agreement.

The following are examples of closed questions to avoid in general use, unless you do want to stop the person talking, or when summarizing:

- 'Would you agree that . . . . ?'
- 'Is it true that . . . . ?'

- 'Do you think that . . . . ?'
- 'So you believe that . . . . ?'
- 'Do we agree then that . . . . ?'

Examples of closed questions which could be used at the start of the interview:

- 'Are you still all right for time for the interview?'
- 'Did you manage to review your performance against the standards as we agreed?'

The development of the skill in using open, probe and link questions will certainly improve the chances of successful appraisal interviews, as will the correct choice of time to use occasionally the closed question. Unfortunately there are other types of questions which many people seem to have a tendency to use and they seldom work favourably towards the achievement of meaningful objectives. The questions in this category can be described as 'leading', 'evaluative' and 'limited choice'.

LEADING QUESTIONS

Leading questions indicate the answer expected or required, and most of the time their use is unfair. The interviewer may not only discover very little about the interviewee's own views, but also force out a misleading or antagonistic response. For example:

- 'Don't you think that the attitude of younger staff today leaves much to be desired?'

EVALUATIVE QUESTIONS

Evaluative questions or responses include the interviewer's opinion with regard to the interviewee's statement. This is often made worse by commenting before the full picture is revealed. For example:

- 'Don't you think that was rather hasty?'
- 'Surely you don't think that would work?'
- 'Shouldn't you have thought about the obvious reper-cussions?

Apart from anything else, it is unlikely that this kind of response will stimulate further good conversation. Should it be considered necessary to establish whether the interviewee thought the action taken was best or not, an open question like 'Faced with similar circumstances again, what action would you take?' would be more appropriate.

LIMITED-CHOICE QUESTIONS

Limited-choice questions are, as the name implies, questions which can be answered only within the limits the questioner has set. For example:

- 'Shall we send you on a three-day or a five-day training course?' There may be many more options open that would meet the objective!
- 'Are you going to talk to Jim about his appearance or shall I?' It is possible that a more viable solution exists!

Restricting your statement to signposts to keep the interview on track; avoiding the tendency to use leading, evaluative and limited choice questions; and developing your skill in selecting and phrasing open, probe, link and closed questions, will undoubtedly work towards a good open interchange of views, but to be really successful the skill of listening has to be developed.

Listening is the most neglected of communication skills. A great deal of effort goes into teaching managers to talk and write effectively, but there is much less attention applied to training people in how to become effective listeners.

88

Listening is the means by which the interviewer learns about the interviewee, but to be really effective it has to go beyond the passive activity of hearing. It requires the desire and ability to listen with understanding—which includes 'listening with the eyes'.

Maintain an active attitude and be on the lookout for words used which appear to conflict with facial expressions. Consider how many ways the phrase 'I agree' can change, dependent upon tone of voice and the expression on the face of the speaker.

Do not be too quick to jump to the conclusion that you understand what it is that has just been said; often we make this leap because of a tendency to compare the statement with our own viewpoint. It is much safer to work on the assumption that you do not fully understand what has been said, and discipline yourself to ask questions to clarify the situation. Do be careful, however, that you do not fall into the trap of the 'insult response'—by seeking clarification to something said by a phrase such as: 'Is this what you are *trying* to say?' It is much more polite, and constructive, to take the responsibility yourself and possibly say, 'Correct me if I'm wrong, but I understand you to be saying . . .', or 'Am I correct in assuming that . . . ?'

People's respect for you will grow when they can see that you are trying to listen more effectively, and a cyclical effect can start here. Effective listening can cause improved relationships, and a good relationship can make listening easier and more effective. The cycle can also go in the opposite direction, however. Poor listening can cause bad relationships, and a bad relationship can make listening more difficult and less effective!

By following the guidelines, and by working hard to develop the skills, your interview can close with an agreed plan of action for improvement.

The plan should be realistic and be based upon examination of the result areas and all aspects which bear on these results; the aim is the removal of problems that restrict performance, or at least the minimization of the effect that these problems have on job results.

It is essential that the plan is specific and spells out precisely the actions required by all persons involved. Vague statements, such as 'a marked improvement is required' or 'information should be more readily available', should be totally avoided.

For the plan to work and provide the expected improvement, it should be based on commitment, not on the manager's ideas being imposed on the employee, or the case of the manager agreeing to certain actions which he or she has little intention of implementing.

The plan should include dates when reviews of progress will be made, and it will help if both the interviewer and the interviewee retain a copy of the plan so that promises have a better chance of becoming commitments. Having said that, if the plan was truly written as a joint effort between yourself and the job holder, you should find that the job holder is much more comfortable working with you to ensure that the agreed actions are taken. All of which adds up to good working relations.

A checklist for improved appraisal interviews

- *Be prepared*, which also includes being prepared to encourage the interviewee to do most of the talking.
- *Concentrate* on the reduction of stress at all times, and this includes both interviewer and interviewee.
- *Statements* should be used only as signposts to remind both of you where you are going.
- *Develop* the skills in selecting and phrasing the questions which encourage the interviewee to talk openly.
- *Be careful* to use only a *closed* question when you want to settle the interviewee down at the start of the interview, to stop the interviewee talking excessively, or in summarizing the interview at the close.
- *Avoid* the use of *leading, evaluative* or *limited-choice* questions.
- *Practise* the skill of listening with understanding.
- *Agree* a plan of action which is realistic to the problems affecting results, is specific to actions required by all, has commitment by both parties, has review dates to check progress, and is copied for both interviewer and interviewee to use.
- *Follow up* the interview immediately with an appraisal of yourself on how you conducted the interview.
- *Follow up* all actions agreed. Never be accused of nothing happening as a result of an appraisal interview.

Appraiser—appraise thyself!

The following questions, if answered immediately after your interview with your employee, will help you to work towards continued improvement in appraisal interviewing.

- How effectively did I listen?
- How often did I interrupt?
- How often did I talk at?
- How often did I ignore suggestions?
- How often did I reject viewpoints?
- Were exchanges frank and open?
- Were comments guarded, or open?
- Was there a readiness to agree?
- Was there any evidence of suspicion?
- How did we tackle 'difficult' areas?
- Did we avoid sensitive areas?
- Did we skate over any difficult issues?
- Did we fully discuss the realities or problems?
- How effectively did I handle conflicting views?
- Did I react by using my authority?
- Did I react emotionally at any point?
- Did I soak up the tension to take the heat out of any situation?
- Did I try to deflate the interviewee or try to score victories at any point?
- How effectively were problems discussed?
- Did we differentiate clearly between causes and effects of the problem discussed?
- Is the job holder now able to achieve the correct standards?
- Does the job holder know how to achieve the standards?
- Does the job holder want to achieve the standards?
- How satisfactory were the physical arrangements?
- Were we interrupted?

- Was the interview curtailed by other pressures?
- How accurate was my assessment of the time the interview required?
- What has the interview done to our relationship?
- What specifically have I learned?
- What have I got to do now with regard to follow-up actions?
- Make a commitment *now* that any problems not foreseen at the time of writing the action plan, are tackled and not just used as a good excuse for doing nothing.

7.

Administration

Periodic planning and review of performance is a critical management responsibility which can have a positive impact on your company's success. If the responsibility is carried out effectively it will enhance communication, improve productivity and stimulate employee development and growth.

Managers who truly support this view do ensure that effort is put into the appraisal process continuously and also on a more formalized basis at regular intervals. They know that certain things can be overlooked when the day-to-day business pressure is on, which is why they combine the informal with the more formal approach to minimize the occurrence. Such managers are usually running efficient and successful departments, but they do appear to be in the minority.

There are other managers who support the idea but find the task difficult to do. They are often troubled by the process and usually dissatisfied with the results, possibly due to inadequate training, but this group makes up a large part of the management population.

A third group of managers is made up from those with a totally negative attitude towards appraisal of any kind; they demand high output from anyone working for them and see appraisal as something extra to their job which they either see no need for, or they simply 'don't have the time!'

Consider the potential problems for a company that has its management team made up from all three of the groups mentioned, and this tends to be the norm for a very large proportion of businesses. There cannot be much comfort for the employees with very little compatibility in the way various departments handle their staff. Not only is it inefficient, it is totally unfair: some people are appraised fairly and effectively; the majority are appraised badly; and some are not appraised at all. This is hardly conducive to harmony and cooperation between departments which should be working towards the achievement of common objectives to enhance the future prospects of the organization as a whole.

There are good reasons, therefore, to recommend that appraisal should be formalized to some extent within the company; each manager's skill in appraising should be monitored; and effective training in this skill should be provided when necessary. Collectively this will have the result of encouraging all managers to be more uniform in the way they manage their staff, the real problem affecting performance will be tackled, more employees will be able to work more effectively towards specific results, and departments will be more able to work in harmony for the good of the company's future growth and security.

The extent to which a company formalizes its appraisal process will be determined by the company's culture and policies. There is little point in imposing any system or documentation which is not in keeping with the company's style. Keeping it simple, however, is a rule which generates the fewest number of administrative problems and makes it easier for all to follow. The purpose of formalizing the appraisal should be borne in mind at all times, remembering that no matter what procedure is chosen it must be an aid to uniform appraisal. Any documentation used should provide the company with more complete records which help the company and the individuals within it. Harmonizing this effort will work towards the achievement of the prime objective of performance appraisal, which must be performance improvement.

Rules of administration

Although the choice of procedure and documentation is individual to the company, there are three rules with regard to the administration which should be considered.

THE FIRST RULE

The first rule applies to frequency. However often performance is discussed with the employee, there is still a case for taking the time to do this more formally on the regular basis of, at the very least, once per year. Ensuring that all managers appraise their employees on a regular basis can provide real benefits:

- All employees will at least be appraised, which covers one aspect of uniformity.
- Providing the 'stock-taking' approach will minimize the likelihood of important issues being overlooked through day-to-day business pressures.
- The ability of each manager to appraise can be monitored.
- Action taken to overcome problems can now be providing an ongoing improvement in all cases, rather than restricting the improvements to the areas under the control of a minority of managers.

THE SECOND RULE

The second rule applies to consistency and quality of appraisal. Irrespective of any training provided to managers, it is not easy to achieve a common standard of understanding with regard to the skills of appraisal, and it is even more difficult to obtain a common standard of enthusiasm towards the process. Guidelines which reduce the chances of personal bias or prejudice are essential if we are to achieve a conformity of quality of appraisal. Each manager in the company must understand what it is that the company is interested in appraising, and must also have a common understanding with regard to the interpretation and recording of information that results in the most appropriate action.

Guidelines can be in the form of a set of questions which have to be covered, together with explanatory notes or sample answers. It is vital that management at all levels is involved in the design of any such documentation and supporting guidelines, and also with the procedure to be employed, although the degree of managerial involvement will depend upon the size and nature of the organization.

THE THIRD RULE

The third rule applies to ownership. Performance appraisal will become really effective when each manager accepts the responsibility for it. In companies that have a personnel department, the responsibility for the coordination of appraisals is often placed there. It should be remembered, however, that this responsibility is the provision of a service to the company and its departments. For example, a personnel department may have the responsibility to remind managers of the dates agreed for periodic reviews. It may also be asked to analyse the total number of completed appraisal forms, to determine the company's overall training or development needs and how these may best be met. The provision of this service does not take any responsibility away from other managers in the company with regard to conducting appraisals for their employees, and ensuring that agreed action is taken.

After all, as a manager you are judged by the performance of the people who work for you. It seems only reasonable, therefore, to accept the responsibility to ensure that every person who works for you has every opportunity to improve.

Guidelines for periodic appraisal

These guidelines describe an approach to periodic performance appraisal which should ensure fairness and consistency for all concerned. Consideration has been given to the most commonly experienced difficulties in the appraisal of employees. The guidelines, where used in conjunction with the contents of the previous chapters, are designed to help you to carry out this most important management responsibility. Success will depend on your support and hard work, but the return on this investment of effort will make it well worth your while.

The approach stresses a total process that is based on a clear mutual understanding of the performance expected, when you and your employees have agreed realistic and measurable work objectives. Appraisal emphasis must be placed on these job-related results, where the main objective is to recognize and encourage the positive aspects of performance and work towards improvement in areas where change is needed. Any appraisal documents used should ensure that fairness can prevail by restricting the information to those areas of the employee's job which contribute most to the company's overall success, thereby avoiding the risk of assessing people on personality traits that have no impact on results.

A formal appraisal of performance should be carried out regularly. The decision relating to the precise length of the review period will depend on prevailing circumstances within the company, but it should not be greater than twelve calendar months and should be the same for all employees. The only exception to similar review periods for all will be for people in new positions, where more regular reviews will be needed. The review should provide a record of results achieved, an evaluation of how well they were carried out in the light of external constraints and, where required, an overall rating of performance.

The way the appraisal form is completed should be the way you would normally communicate with the employee being appraised. Consistency is essential and personal prejudices should not be allowed to influence the statements. Simple factual comments are all that are required provided they are accurate descriptions of what has been achieved, and with what success. Your employee will wish to read what you have written, so agreement and understanding are critical.

Similarly, your own manager may wish to review the document so there must be sufficient data to support your recommended action, and any subsequent ratings where they are seen to be necessary.

It is not the author's intention to specify the design of any documentation for your company, neither is it his intention to say how guidelines should be written. But as an illustration of how the two can be used to improve the effectiveness of periodic appraisal, an example of guidance notes can be seen in Appendix 2, and an example of an appraisal form is shown in Appendix 3.

The appraisal form used in the example, Appendix 3, has seven interdependent sections. Sections A and B cover the job holder's personal details and career history. Section C, covers:

1. the vital key tasks associated with each main result area;
2. the defined standards of performance which have previously been agreed;
3. the actual performance achieved against each task.

This section records major performance results achieved during the period under review using quantitative measurement. To ensure a fair and balanced assessment all five result areas must be taken into consideration, i.e. finance, communication, staff development, supervision, and the specialism. Make sure that specific end results achieved are identified rather than simply listing the activities with which the person has been involved. This section should be completed by showing how each of the results achieved compares with the standard agreed at the beginning of the period under review. Once again it is essential that quantitative statements are used, and that all results planned for are accurately stated in terms of results.

As no blame or credit is being attached to these statements at this point, it is essential that only the true description of the actual results is quoted. Do not be tempted to make allowances because things have been tough or easy over the period under review; this will be taken into consideration in section D.

Section D deals with prevailing conditions which could affect results. All considerations, both inside the job itself and in the job surrounds, have to be considered here to ascertain the true extent of the employee's control over the situation. It would be totally unfair to ignore environmental factors that are having more impact on the results than the employee's own influence. A proper analysis of the differences between desired and actual performance will provide information with regard to the most likely cause of any discrepancy. If this is verified during the interview with the employee, the most appropriate action can then be agreed, whether this is the provision of training or the removal of an obstacle. However, when it is discovered that an employee's performance has been adversely influenced by conditions outside his or her control, your comments on how the person handled the difficulty will help in the overall assessment.

Section E provides the opportunity to comment with regard to the amount of direct supervision which was required, in order to achieve the results specified in section C.

Section F collects feedback from the job holder which will assist in company planning.

Section G deals with actions required to achieve improved performance with the opportunity to agree new standards of performance.

It is strongly recommended that both the job holder and the appraising manager leave the interview with a copy of the agreed plan of action (section G). This will be followed up by both parties.

In a Utopian situation section G could be left blank! But more realistically it is essential that it is completed and contains information in the form of a specific plan of action aimed at the improvements needed. Alternatively, the action may be geared to a greater utilization of skills and abilities by further development.

A tendency to be avoided when developing action plans is to work on the fairly natural assumption that the action required will always be in the area of training the employee. While this can be true in some cases, it is much more productive to look back at the previous sections where there may be information that suggests otherwise. To help you in this regard, it is strongly recommended that the completion of this section does not take place until the interview with the employee is well under way. This will allow you to include his or her inputs; ironically, job holders do seem at times to have more information than their managers.

Concentrating on the three aspects of potential need will more often aid you to achieve your objective:

1. What specific skill or knowledge is lacking?
2. What obstacles outside the job either have to be removed, or their impact on the job reduced?
3. In what way have you, as the manager, to change in the way you are managing this employee?

RATING OF PERFORMANCE

Rating performance on an annual basis is an administrative necessity in some companies, although it is not recommended unless those on high have decreed that it will be done. Successful appraisal interviews usually finish with agreement on actions to be taken, until the subject of ratings surfaces. However, if you have been told by people who obviously know best that a ratings system will be used, for whatever purpose, it has to be used as objectively as is possible.

Rating systems are often used to provide an input for salary administration, a measurable record of achievement, a recognition of accomplishment and an indicator of improvement required. Performance ratings are sometimes factors affecting promotion or dismissal. It is, therefore, critical that ratings are assigned with careful judgement and in accordance with information contained in the preceding sections.

A word of caution! Your work done in completing the sections in the appraisal form may or may not be complete or accurate. Your interview with the employee may reveal more information; with this in mind you may consider a provisional rating before the interview, but the final decision must be made after the employee has had a real opportunity to clarify fully the situation.

When ratings are used it is essential that individuals are rated on their performance in their job against clearly defined and agreed standards, and not by comparison with the performance of others, which could be a very unfair comparison; ratings must be fair or a disservice will be done to the individual and to the company. Acquiring complete and accurate performance data is the only way that a truly representative rating can be determined.

The approach recommended is for you to select, from the categories listed below, the option which most accurately describes the employee's performance. This involves your judgement but it should be as objective as possible. The comments on the form must substantiate the rating chosen by providing the facts upon which the judgement was made.

The ratings available to choose from are simply numbered one to six, the best rating being number one.

Rating number one will be selected when results show that performance is the best that can be attained. All standards are consistently met and achievement is at an accelerated rate. Contribution to the organization is distinguished and above expectation. Minimal supervision and counsel are required.

Rating number two will apply when it can be shown that performance is superior, objectives are generally met and achievement is of a high standard even on complex tasks. Contribution to the organization is significant and a limited amount of supervision and direction are required.

Rating number three will be most appropriate when results show that performance is completely satisfactory and the majority of the important standards are achieved. Contribution to the organization is that to be expected from a person in this position. Normal supervision and counsel required.

Rating number four will apply when performance is just acceptable with the achievement of several important standards. Some objectives are not fully achieved but improvement and development can be planned and achieved. More than normal guidance and supervision are required.

Rating number five should be chosen when it can be seen that performance is not acceptable because very few important standards are being met. An abnormal amount of supervision is required to maintain any real contribution to the organization. Specific improvement must be achieved by a specific date to justify continued employment at the current job level.

Rating number six will apply only when the person has had insufficient time in the present position to make a judgement fair.

Numbers were chosen to represent different ratings rather than descriptive words which could be very ambiguous. Nevertheless, the above descriptions can still be misleading, and for this reason you are asked to check your selected ratings with the following three tests before commitment: validity, reliability and fairness.

VALIDITY

Is the rating selected a valid measurement of total job performance?

Ratings based on actual performance as measured against the stated requirements or standards of performance will usually meet the test of validity.

Judgements of personality factors, assumed skill level, education, intelligence or other similar factors are most difficult to relate to job performance. These factors have different meanings to different people, and although there may be reasons for good or bad performance it must be the demonstrated performance that is being rated and not the person's assumed ability.

The overall rating should take the following into consideration.

- Total versus partial results.
- Major versus minor accomplishments.
- Demonstrated and observed behaviour which aided or hindered others.
- The total pattern of results; was performance consistent in all areas?
- Were there significant instances of very positive results or real omissions?
- Did results conform to what was agreed?
- To what extent did results meet specified standards of quality and quantity?

RELIABILITY

Is the rating selected reliable in that other managers in a similar situation would give the same rating?

The reliability of a rating can be damaged by a number of factors. Among these are the strictness or leniency of a manager's own standards or certain personal biases. While it is true that you should set high standards, you should apply them equally to all individuals in similar positions. You should also compare your standards of expectation with other managers in a similar position to yourself.

The reliability of a rating is questionable when:

- everyone seems to come out with the same rating;
- one incident causes an undue influence on other areas of performance;
- individuals are ranked against one another;
- individuals are rated against future potential;
- a lower rating is given 'to give room to show improvement next year'.

FAIRNESS

Is the rating fair, in that it takes into account circumstances beyond the employee's control?

A rating system should not deteriorate into a 'by the book' approach that loses sight of the reason for which it is carried out. Valid reasons may exist for missing planned results and tolerance for circumstances should be included, for example:

- Were all conditions beyond the employee's control taken into consideration?
- In retrospect, was the workload over-ambitious?
- Is the problem in the performance plan or in the performance itself?

- Are minor shortcomings in one area offset by strengths in performance in another area?
- Was some leeway allowed for in the standards or in retrospect were they too rigid or incorrect?

To summarize on ratings, there are five essential steps which must be taken:

1. Review the total performance and note any areas that stand above or fall below the agreed standard.
2. Identify the most likely causes of any differences.
3. Check steps one and two with your employee.
4. Weigh up the total situation.
5. Select a rating that best describes the employee's performance.

THE FINAL TEST

You will have to be able to explain precisely to your employee, and to your own manager, without argument why the chosen rating applies!

8.

Identification of potential

Many companies which carry out performance appraisal also keep records on the potential of their employees for future promotion opportunities. While this is very commendable, as a good appraisal approach can provide valuable information about a person's apparent potential, it can be very damaging to assume that the link between the two is naturally strong.

The task of identifying potential for promotion cannot be easy for the appraising manager, since competence of a member of staff to perform well in the current job is not an automatic indicator of potential for promotion. Too often the first-class salesperson is promoted to become a mediocre sales manager, the excellent chief engineer is promoted to become a very poor engineering director, and the star football player struggles to be a football team manager.

Before being accused of suggesting that good performers must stay where they are, which is not always true, let us take a look at the problem from a different angle.

Potential can be defined as 'a latent but unrealized ability', but why is it so often assumed that this latent ability should always be directed towards promotion? There are many people who have the desire and the potential to advance through the job they are in, wanting the opportunity to operate at a higher level of competence in the same type of work. This potential is the one that the appraising manager should be able to identify and develop because of knowledge of the job.

To expect appraising managers to be able to identify and develop potential for promotion is a different matter. This requires an in-depth study of the positions which may become vacant, looking carefully at the specific skills that the new position may demand, and also, taking into consideration the more subjective areas like 'qualities required'. These may be areas where the employee has not had a real opportunity to demonstrate potential ability, and they may be areas with which you, as the appraising manager, are not familiar.

However, as its manager you can assist your company in this important activity through your knowledge of your staff. To enable you to be more confident in your advice the following indicators should be looked for during your day-to-day contact with your employees, as they do appear to be some of the characteristics seen in individuals who have high potential for promotion.

INDICATORS OF POTENTIAL

A sense of reality This is the extent to which a person thinks and acts objectively, resisting purely emotional pressures but pursuing realistic projects with enthusiasm.

Imagination/creativity The ability to let the mind range over a wide variety of possible courses of action; going beyond the conventional approaches to situations and not being confined to 'This is the way it's always been done!'

Power of analysis The capacity to break down, reformulate or transform a complicated situation into manageable terms.

Breadth of vision The ability to examine a problem in the context of a much broader framework of reference; being able to detect, within a specific situation, relationships with those aspects which could be affecting the situation.

Persuasiveness The ability to sell ideas to other people and gain a continuing commitment, particularly when the individual is using personal influence rather than 'management authority'.

Empathy The demonstrated ability to understand fully other people's feelings, and evidence that the person knows how to use this information to the benefit of as many people as possible.

Judgement The faculty of being able to make critical distinctions, and achieve a balanced viewpoint.

Flexibility Not having too many fixed ideas on how situations should be tackled, and recognition that people and situations may not be the same from day to day.

Personal drive A sense of ambition to achieve results. The ability and desire to work with the minimum of supervision.

Any organization needs to make the best use of its most valuable asset, which is good people; successful companies make sure that this is done!

If we all put extra effort into ensuring that talent and potential are identified, developed, and above all utilized, we will be doing our job as managers and we will be making sure that whoever replaces us, when the time comes, will be better than we ever were.

9.

Personal application

Table 9.1 lists a number of vital key tasks which may, or may not, be associated with the five main result areas within your job role. There is space alongside these for you to describe the required standard of performance.

To help you to identify the vital key tasks specific to your job, in other words those which will influence your achievement of given objectives, do go through the list, delete those which do not relate to your job, but add others which you believe should have appeared.

Now looking at each vital key task in turn, determine what you consider to be a required standard of performance. Chapter 2 will assist you in this task, but the person who should be best able to advise you will be your immediate manager. Do ask for that person's involvement – it is as much in that person's interests as anyone else.

Table 9.1   Personal application of vital key tasks

Vital key tasks	Standards of performance
Finance	
Budget development	
Budget maintenance	
Quality costs	
Labour costs (and overtime costs)	
Profitability/margins	
. . . .	
. . . .	
. . . .	
. . . .	
Supervision	
Selection of personnel	
Organization of the team	
Individual direction	
Motivation	
Appraisal of the staff	
General discipline	
Safety	
Throughput of work	
Labour turnover	
Overtime worked	
. . . .	
. . . .	
Communication	
Reports	
Letter-writing	
Meetings	
Keeping people informed, i.e. your staff, customers, suppliers, other departments	
Making presentations	

Table 9.1   Personal application of vital key tasks (*cont.*)

Vital key tasks	Standards of performance
....	
....	
....	
....	

Staff development
Training of staff to improve current
performance
Training of staff for new assignments
Extent of delegation
Extent of coverage for own function
Extent of coverage for specific duties
Length of time department can be left
unsupervised
Amount of advanced warning needed if
department is going to be left
....
....

Specialism
Market penetration
New products developed
New products sold
Profitability of new products
New products on line
New processes installed
Quality
Work flow
Recruitment
Training
Sales demonstrations
Discount obtained

Table 9.1 (*cont.*)

Vital key tasks	*Standards of performance*
Sales margins	
Month end balances	
Cash flow situations	
Debtors	
Project management	
Systems management	
Turnover growth	
Service reliability	
User acceptability	
Maintenance of records	
. . . .	
. . . .	
. . . .	
. . . .	
. . . .	

Appendix 1

Preparation by the job holder for the appraisal discussion

Performance appraisal is an important key in helping the job holder to integrate his/her own personal objectives with those of the job and the company.

These notes are intended to assist you in preparing for the performance appraisal discussion with your manager/supervisor.

The main purpose of that discussion is for you and your manager to jointly discuss the standards agreed for the main elements of your job and objectively review how well you have carried them out. It is also an opportunity to consider what may be done to remove any difficulties which have inadvertently been built into your job, develop your capabilities and to agree the standards for the following period.

As an aid to your preparation we give you the following series of questions. It is left to you whether you use the form or not. These notes are for your personal use only and you may keep or destroy them as you wish. You may, of course, use them at the interview itself, but there are no requirements for you to do so.

The more time spent on preparation increases the opportunity of gaining the following benefits:

- Opportunity to find out own strengths
- Opportunity to find out own weaknesses
- Opportunity to discuss own objectives
- Opportunity to discuss objectives of company/department

- Opportunity to discuss future/prospects
- Opportunity to express own views
- Indication of own role
- Improve working relationships
- Increase job satisfaction
- Improve self-confidence
- Opportunity to analyse objectively any difficulties
- See relationship to any training provided
- See relationship to development plans

1. What do you feel have been the most important tasks in your present job during the period of this review? . . . .
. . . .
. . . .

2. As you see it:
   (a) Describe how you feel you have performed in your job, during the period under review: . . . .
   . . . .
   . . . .

   (b) What difficulties (if any) have you encountered with regard to aspects of the job which are outside your control? . . . .
   . . . .
   . . . .

   (c) In what way would you improve your performance, where necessary? . . . .
   . . . .
   . . . .

3. How would you summarize your performance? Consider not only what you have achieved, but the way you have achieved it: . . . .
. . . .
. . . .

4. In your opinion, what action do you feel should be taken to assist you in performing your job to the best of your capabilities in the coming year?
   (a) By you: . . . .
   (b) By your supervisor: . . . .

(c) By other people? . . . .

5. In terms of results describe your main strengths and weaknesses: . .
. . . .

6. In most jobs, there are some things we find more interesting than others:

(a) What do you like most in your present job? . . . .
. . . .

(b) What do you like the least? . . . .
. . . .

(c) In what way could your capabilities be better used? . . . .
. . . .
. . . .

7. Are there aspects of the job which you find unsatisfactory or points on which you would like more information? . . . .
. . . .
. . . .

8. What steps, if any, are you taking in personal development (languages, management or trade associated courses)? . . . .
. . . .

9. Are there any constraints on future developments (domestic, mobility, health, personal etc.)? . . . .
. . . .

10. What special training or experience, if any, would you need in order to improve further your performance? . . . .
. . . .

Appendix 2

Performance Appraisal Procedure and guidance notes

1. Introduction

Performance appraisal is an important key to successful management. It provides the opportunity for managers to stand back from day-to-day events and review with individuals, past performance and future aims, integrating the job holder's personal objectives with those of the job and the company.

2. Purpose

The Performance Appraisal Procedure has been designed to assist managers to hold constructive, free and open discussions with their job holders in order that agreement can be reached on:

(a) present and future objectives;
(b) the level of performance achieved by the individual;
(c) any action necessary to improve performance.

The Performance Appraisal Form provides the necessary discipline to ensure that the discussion is comprehensive and objective. It also provides a record so that agreed action plans can be implemented and monitored during the following year. In addition it includes a section where the individual can state his or her views on organizational development. The job holders' preparation forms are intended to help them prepare in advance for the discussion, in particular to give consideration to the main aspects of the job and to carry out some self-assessment of performance and future training and development needs. However, it is the job holder's choice whether to use the form or not.

The time invested reading the following notes in preparation for the interview should yield these benefits to the manager.

THE OPPORTUNITY TO:

- improve performance of individuals
- improve performance of departments
- improve communication
- improve relationships
- identify staff weaknesses
- identify staff strengths
- identify potential problems
- identify any existing problems
- identify departmental training needs
- identify departmental development
- identify potential
- discover own strengths and weaknesses
- discover areas to increase delegation
- communicate department/company objectives
- praise/correct
- information related to job satisfaction
- information related to training received
- information relating to employees' attitudes
- demonstrate managerial skills
- help develop job holder's talents
- clarify responsibilities
- prevent the recurrence of difficulties

3. Responsibilities of the manager

In the following and all Performance Appraisal documentation, anybody who has responsibility for staff is referred to as the manager, the person whose performance is being appraised is referred to as the job holder, and the manager's manager who is responsible for ensuring the commonality of procedure and the final signing of the form is referred to as the reviewing manager.

The responsibilities of the manager are as follows:

(a) Conduct an appraisal discussion **once per year** and, in the case of a new employee, on the date of their official review (managers are encouraged to carry out informal discussion more frequently).

(b) Arrange a date and time for the discussion and give the job holder a copy of the notes entitled, 'Preparation by the Job Holder, for the Appraisal Discussion' at least five working days before the discussion is due to take place.

(c) Complete the indicated sections before the discussion.

(d) Carry out the discussion as informally as possible, free from interruptions and in a familiar but private place.

(e) Complete the appraisal form in its entirety during the interview, obtain the reviewing manager's signature, show it to the job holder, agree any amendments as necessary, sign it and ask the job holder to sign it.

(f) A copy of the completed action plan is to be retained by the job holder and the appraising manager, with dates for actions and review meetings and revised standards of performance. The remaining document must be treated in the strictest confidence and securely filed in the designated place. Sight of the document can be extended to more senior members of management upon request.

(g) Follow up any agreed action plans during the year as specified.

(h) Before conducting the interview allocate sufficient time to cover all the points, allowing extra time for any unanticipated subjects being raised.

4. Completion of the Performance Appraisal Form

SECTION A AND SECTION B

Both these sections on Personal Details and Career History should be completed before the interview by the Personnel Department or the appraising manager accordingly. It is well worth running through the details at the beginning of the interview, to check the accuracy of the information.

SECTION C

All three columns should be completed before the interview.

In the left column **Vital Key Tasks** should be stated for each main result area. The selection of these must be influenced by their importance rather than ease of measurement and must be representative on the full span of the job.

In a more junior position only two or three of the five result areas may apply.

In the middle column the **Standards of Performance** relating to the **Vital Key Tasks** should be stated. These will have been established at the last interview/review.

* If this is the first appraisal, we recommend a meeting for setting the standards prior to the interview. These standards should be acceptable to all concerned as this adds to the commitment, using information from the past, present and future. They should be valid in terms of results and realistic in terms of achievement. Strive for clear definitions.

In the right column the **Actual Performance** relating to the adjacent **Standards of Performance** should be stated. This you will have been recording since the last interview/review.

* If this is the first appraisal the **Actual Performance** may be difficult to state and gain agreement on from the job holder, as the standard may not have been set at the beginning of the period under review.

Take steps before the interview to analyse the differences (if any) between the agreed and the actual performance, and note the perceived causes of these differences.

Discuss all three columns with job holders during the interview, to obtain their views on each.

SECTION D

During the interview it is advised that you make notes on a separate piece of paper of any obstacles outside/within the job holder's control that have inadvertently been built into the job. Then complete section D by condensing these through discussion, establishing their validity and entering each problem area against its relevant function. The discussion should be solely about the facts in section C, coupled with whatever self-appraisal information the job holder has divulged, encouraging each person to highlight these problem areas.

SECTION E

This section should be completed during the interview by referring to the information gathered in sections C and D and your observation from your day-to-day contact with the job holder regarding the amount of supervision and counselling required. When completing this section ensure that the information is:

- **relevant**   to the performance standards previously agreed;
- **complete** in that the information should cover the **entire** period under review leaving no gaps;
- **explicit**   in that it will determine both whether the agreed standards have been met, and the true extent of any shortfall; and
- **accurate** as distorted information will most likely result in an uncomfortable interview, which will fail to gain agreement on those follow-up actions.

SECTION F

Items 1–3

These questions are simply fact-finding on feedback information the job holders may have considered during their preparation to be interviewed. Its purpose is for company planning.

Item 4

Allow the job holder to freely comment on any aspect of the appraisal, and note all relevant comments.

SECTION G

This section should be completed at the end of the interview with the job holder.

Item 1

State action to be taken by the job holder, the appraising manager and any other person included, with dates when actions should be taken by. The result of these actions should assist the job holder in attaining or improving the **Standard of Performance** required. They will be in the form of training, removal of obstacles or changes required.

Item 2

State the **Revised Standards of Performance** against the **Vital Key Tasks** stated in section C for each result area. These should continue to be agreed, valid, realistic but challenging and well defined.

Item 3

Agree a date for reviewing the progress and to check that the relevant actions have taken place.

Item 4

Obtain the reviewing manager's signature, show it to the job holder, agree any amendments where necessary, date it, sign it and ask the job holder to sign it.

NOTE: A copy of the action plan is to be retained by the appraising manager and the job holder.

Appendix 3

Performance Appraisal Form

Note: *Before starting this Performance Appraisal Form, the Appraiser should read the relevant Guidance Notes.*

A. Personal Details—Complete before Interview

Job Holder's Name:
Job Title:
Department/Location:
Appraiser's Name and Title:
Period under Review:
Date of this Appraisal: *Date of last Appraisal:*   *Conducted by:*

B. Career History—Complete before Interview

Date Job Holder joined Company:
Time Job Holder has spent in current job:
Last three appointments held (within the Company or before joining the Company)

SECTION C   Complete before Interview

VITAL KEY TASKS *(Against the 5 main result areas)*	MEASURABLE STANDARDS OF PERFORMANCE AGREED
FINANCE:	
SUPERVISION:	
COMMUNICATION:	
STAFF DEVELOPMENT:	
SPECIALISM:	

SECTION D **Complete during Interview**

ACTUAL PERFORMANCE   *What obstacles outside/within the Job Holder's control have been established during the interview?*

SECTION E   Complete during Interview

> *1. What percentage of time was given for direct supervision in attaining actual performance (consider the obstacles in section D)?*

SECTION F   Complete during Interview

> *1. What is the Job Holder's opinion with regard to areas where he or she feels the company could improve as an organization?*

> *2. What steps are being taken by the Job Holder, if any, in personal development (languages, management or trade associated courses)?*

> *3. Are there any constraints on future development (domestic, mobility, health, personal etc.)?*

> *4. Job Holder's comments:*

SECTION G   Complete on Conclusion of Interview

ACTION PLAN
*Copy of this section should
be given to Job Holder*

---

1. What action has to be taken in terms of training, development, removal of obstacles, or changes by the following people?	*2. REVISED STANDARDS OF PERFORMANCE*
a.1. the Appraising a.2. when by? *Manager:*	*Finance*
	Supervision
b.1. the Job b.2. when by? *Holder:*	*Communication*

c.1. any other   c.2. when by?
       person
       involved:
	Staff Development

	Specialism

---

3. What is the agreed review date to check on progress? . . . .

---

4. Signature of Reviewing
    Manager . . . . *Date* . . . .

   Signature of Appraising
   Manager . . . . *Date* . . . .

   Signature of Job Holder . . . . *Date* . . . .

Index